Entrepreneur.
MAGAZINE'S

ULTIMATE

BOOK OF

SALES

LETTERS

Customize Your Letters, Memos,
E-mails and Presentations
with the Enclosed CD-ROM

CHERYL KIMBALL and JONI VAN GELDER

EP
Entrepreneur. Press

Editorial Director: Jere Calmes

Acquisitions Editor: Karen Thomas

Cover Design: Beth Hansen-Winter

Production and Editorial Services: CWL Publishing Enterprises, Inc., Madison, Wisconsin, www.cwlpub.com.

This publication is designed to provide accurate and authoritative information in regard to the subject matter covered. It is sold with the understanding that the publisher is not engaged in rendering legal, accounting, or other professional services. If legal advice or other expert assistance is required, the services of a competent professional person should be sought.

> —From a Declaration of Principles jointly adopted by
> a Committee of the American Bar Association and
> a Committee of Publishers and Associations

ISBN 13: 978-1-932531-75-6
   10: 1-932531-75-0

Library of Congress Cataloging-in-Publication Data

Kimball, Cheryl.
   Ultimate book of sales letters : customize your letters, memos, e-mails and presentations with the enclosed CD-ROM / by Cheryl Kimball and Joni van Gelder.
      p. cm.
   ISBN 13: 978-1-932531-75-6 (alk. paper)
   ISBN 10: 1-932531-75-0 (alk. paper)
   1. Sales letters—Handbooks, manuals, etc. 2. Commercial correspondence—Handbooks, manuals, etc. I. Van Gelder, Joni. II. Title.

   HF5730.K48 2007
   658.8'1—dc22

                                                    2007002748

Printed in Canada
11 10 09 08 07   10 9 8 7 6 5 4 3 2 1

Contents

Preface   vii

Part 1. Basics of Selling   *1*
   Introduction   1
   Letter vs. Phone Call   1
   Other Choices   2
   The Legal Side of Letter Writing   4
   Delivery Options   4

  1. **Basic Sales Planning Strategy**   7
   Sales Force   7
   Your Message   9
   Alleviate Objections   9
   Timing   9

  2. **Sales Letter Style**   10
   Grammar   11
   In Style   13
   The Paperless Office?   11
   Some Examples   12

  3. **Sales Letter Basics**   15
   Letterhead   15
   Format   15
   The Paperless Office?   17

  4. **Fax/Memo/E-Mail Basics**   18
   Memo Basics   18
   Fax Basics   19
   E-Mail Basics   21

Part 2. Letters for Prospecting   *31*

  5. **Letters of Introduction**   27
   Introduce the Company   27
   Introduce New Products   28
   Introduce a New Service   28
   Announce a Special Sale   28
   Announce a Seasonal Special   28
   Announce a New Sales Person or a Promotion   28
   Models   30–58

6. **Letters to Prospects** — **59**
   Prospects Vs. Existing Customers — 59
   Serendipity — 59
   Direct Mail Lists — 60
   Your Own List — 60
   Using Existing Customers to Prospect — 60
   Mix It Up — 60
   Tailor Your Letters — 60
   A Plan — 61
   Models — 62–85

7. **Letters Requesting a Sales Appointment** — **86**
   Personal Contact — 86
   The Benefit — 86
   The Literature — 87
   Suggest Times — 87
   Their Place or Yours — 87
   Specials — 87
   Helping Them — 87
   Letter Style — 87
   Models — 88–101

8. **Cover Letters** — **102**
   Keep It Simple — 102
   Tone — 102
   In Closing — 103
   Models — 104–115

9. **Sales Proposal Letters** — **116**
   Coupons — 116
   Special Offers — 116
   Solicited Proposals — 116
   Unsolicited Proposals — 117
   Models — 118–139

10. **Follow-up Letters** — **140**
    Literature — 140
    Specifics — 140
    Counter Objections — 140
    Short and Sweet — 141
    After the Sale — 141
    Models — 142–149

Part 3. Letters for Sales Operation — *151*

9. **Sales Letters** — **153**
   Be Honest — 153
   Closing the Sale — 154
   Models — 155–174

12. **Customer Service Letters**   **175**
      Still Keep It Short   175
      Different Kinds of Letters   175
      Surveys   176
      Models   177–203

13. **Letters, E-mails, and Memos for Sales Management**   **204**
      Content   204
      Letters   204
      Memos   205
      E-mail   205
      Models   206–241

14. **Letters for Promotion to Sale Support**   **242**
      Promotion Letter   242
      Press Releases   242
      Letters to the Editor   243
      Models   244–269

15. **Letters to Third Parties**   **270**
      Distributors   270
      Promotional Partners   270
      Chambers of Commerce   270
      Mailing List Brokers   271
      Advertising Agencies   271
      Models   272–291

16. **International Sales Letters**   **292**
      You Say Potato–I Say Potahto   292
      Idioms   293
      The Value of Simplicity   293
      Some Formatting Details   293
      Salutation   294
      The Soft Sell   294
      Models   296–309

Appendix. Check Your Proofreading Ability!   **311**

Preface

The purpose of this book is to make you a better letter/memo/e-mail/fax writer. It provides guidelines and principles for each type of written business communication you're likely to encounter in your worklife. Written communication varies depending on purpose, recipient, context, and situation. If your letter or memo has the wrong tone, you might not get the response you're looking for.

In verbal communication, well over half of your meaning comes from body language, tone of voice, and words chosen. In written communication, meaning is also derived from more than the words that appear on paper. Some situations require formality, others are informal. Some recipients may know a lot about the context of the communication; others have little background on what you're writing about. Ultimately this book will teach you to effectively get your point across in nearly every type of sales situation.

Part 1 provides an overview of the basic types of written sales communication situations you'll deal with, and includes chapters sales letter strategies, style, format, and e-mail and fax basics with selected examples. You may think you know these principles already, but it's still a good review, and we think you might find a few nuggets that will help you improve the quality of your written messages, regardless of the medium you choose.

Parts 2 and 3 form the heart of this book. These parts include model letters you can use or adapt for your particular business.

Part 2 contains letters for prospecting. It includes six chapters on the various aspects of identifying and dealing with new customers. There are models of letters of introduction, prospecting, setting up an appointment, cover letters, proposal letters, and the important follow-up letters. All of these letters include marginal notes explaining or commenting on the hows and whys of each example.

Part 3 is the longest part and provides guidance on letters for all aspects of sales operations. You'll find 15 to 30 model letters in each of these chapters that you can use and adapt.

In addition to the letters in Parts 2 and 3, the accompanying CD includes all those in the book plus hundreds more that you can load onto your computer and adapt as appropriate. This disk will save you hours of time in not having to reinvent the wheel to communicate with customers in every type of sales sitaution.

Part 1

Basics of Selling

Introduction

Whether you are an on-the-ground salesperson or you are the manager of several salespeople, sales letters are going to be a critical part of your business. Despite the electronic age, a good old-fashioned letter that is brief, gets right to the point, yet is friendly and clearly shows the benefit to the reader is more likely to get read. E-mails are easy to delete; not only are cold phone calls less and less welcome in the busy world of today's consumer but things like "caller ID" let people easily avoid any call they aren't sure they want to receive.

Letter vs. Phone Call

Even if consumers were more receptive to cold phone calls these days, a letter still has lots of advantages:

- Letters let you slowly introduce yourself and your product or service to the potential buyer. The buyer gets the chance to learn about what you're offering in the timeframe that works for him or her.

- You can't be hung up on! If you manage to get by caller ID or a secretary or a "Tele-zapper," when a prospect picks up the phone to answer your cold phone call, you have no idea what mood he or she is in and whether the person is extremely busy at that particular moment. If so, your phone call will end abruptly. When people open their mail, they typically wait for a break in their busy day and focus on the task.

- Even if the prospect's mail is opened by someone else, a good sales letter will get passed through to the right person. If you have done your job well in writing your letter and the benefits of what you have to offer are right up front, even the middle person will think the target prospect might want to know about your product. You direct the "conversation" of a sales letter. In a phone call, it's a 50/50 chance who is going to direct the conversation, you or the prospect.

- The letter also gives you the opportunity to forewarn the prospect of your impending call.

But still, you're thinking, write a letter? In the e-mail age? It stills seems like an outdated concept, right? Think again.

Letter writing may be the exception in much day-to-day correspondence, but it is still as important to conducting business as it was in the pre–e-mail era. Written letters provide many benefits:

- First and foremost, written letters are still the best documentation. A letter sent with some form of delivery confirmation is still the best way to prove you communicated with whomever you are trying to communicate with. Sometimes a letter is a legal necessity.

- Written letters are more private and secure than e-mail. Oh, sure, the secretary or your assistant can read a letter. But that is a lot different from an e-mail, which can accidentally, intentionally, or deviously be broadcast to a cast of millions.

- Written letters are without a doubt more professional than e-mail. E-mail by design is intended to be a quick way to communicate something noncritical.

- E-mails are more immediate, yes, but you can always fax a letter if the contents aren't confidential or, if they are, send it overnight, which is still pretty darn fast. If something is important enough to be said faster than overnight mail, you might want to pick up the phone—and follow up with a letter.

- A letter can be a critical component of a sales campaign. In a letter you can take the time you need to support the marketing materials enclosed in the package.

- Even if the correspondence is "in house," a written memo is important in many cases.

Other Choices

Sometimes a letter is not the right choice. For instance,

- If you want something that can be posted on a bulletin board at its final destination, a flyer might be the better way to go—few people want to stand at a bulletin board and read a letter. You will need to get your message across in bulleted lists and short self-contained paragraphs that can be boxed and printed in larger type. A flyer will cost more than a letter since you will probably need to have it printed by an offset printer in order to utilize attractive graphics.

- If you want something to be printed in a publication, the best route is a formal press release. While the press release may sound much like a letter in the long run, newspapers and magazines will expect the piece to be in the form of a press release. You will need to use the specific conventions that apply to press releases.

- If you want to include a coupon or application form, you may want to create something like a trifold brochure. This allows you to include quite a lot of information while still having one of the flaps clippable so it can be sent back as an application or coupon. Again, you will probably need to consider the additional expense of an offset printer for this, depending on how many you plan to do, how sophisticated your computer's publication software is, and how high quality of an office printer you have.

Five Steps to Planning Any Sales Letter

1. Decide what you are hoping to accomplish with the letter.
2. Determine who your prospect is and address the letter to that person.
3. Get to the point. The benefits of your product/service should be right up front, not buried so far in that the reader never gets to the point before tossing the letter in the trash.
4. If your material can be put into a bulleted list, do so. It breaks up the text and makes the reader more inclined to at least browse the entire letter.
5. Be clear in your letter about any follow-up—either by you or by the recipient.

One of the best ways to write effective sales letters is to be extremely comfortable with the products and services you are promoting. Once you get the hang of it, you will enjoy writing letters instead of dreading it.

When Is a Letter Better?

Sometimes e-mail, faxes, memos, or even phone calls work great for conducting business. But many times a letter can often be the best form of communication. Here are 10 of those times:

1. You need to come across in a serious way. Letters with headings, salutations, and sign-offs are very official.
2. What you are saying requires your official signature.
3. The contents of the letter will serve as legal documentation; for example, you are giving a sales representative a warning about his or her poor job performance.
4. You want the contents to be private. Of course, the recipient can choose to spread the letter around, but that can happen accidentally more easily with e-mail and faxes.
5. You want to be formal. No matter how hard you try, your choice of words and tone will probably always be more formal in a letter. Faxes are by nature cryptic and e-mails are by nature informal.
6. You want the information to be easily retrievable in the future. Although the letter may not be as formal as legal documentation, a letter can be easily filed and readily accessed later if necessary. And you can reuse it as a template.

7. Letters can make the recipient feel very special. In our fast-paced society where we can communicate with breakneck speed, a letter still says "this was written especially for you"—even if you sent out a mass mailing of thousands of them!

8. You would like a letter in reply. Sending a letter can give the expectation that you expect the response to be a letter in return.

9. You've tried other means of communication to no avail. Sometimes you've attempted to get across your message in a phone conversation, but the person just isn't hearing it. Or you sent an e-mail, but got no response. A letter, especially if it is sent certified, will capture the attention of the recipient, who will probably read it closely and now get your message.

10. You want the recipient to carefully consider the information you are providing. How many times have you, or someone you have communicated with, read an e-mail and found later that you missed some key points? A letter encourages the reader to read as slowly as he or she wants, and go over each point making sure they understand the message.

Keep file folders on your computer of all the letters you write, even if you use the templates in this book or on the enclosed CD. You will be tailoring them to suit your situations and you can use a lot of the same language again and again.

TIP

The Legal Side of Letter Writing

There is probably not a thing you commit to print that you shouldn't expect could someday, intentionally or by accident, become public or be subpoenaed as evidence in court. Conduct written correspondence (electronic or on paper) with that in mind.

If you have any inkling that a letter spells potential legal trouble, have it read by a lawyer. It just isn't worth taking the chance. Some letters that you should definitely get legal help with are:

- Letters terminating employees
- Letters reprimanding employees that state negative consequences for continued poor performance
- Letters responding to lawsuit threats
- Letters responding to safety complaints of your product, service, or business
- Letters responding to employees or former employees involving sexual harassment, discrimination, or dissatisfaction of any kind

Delivery Options

Writing a letter can be your most effective means of communication, but in order for that to be so, the recipient needs to actually receive the letter! You need to choose the most appropriate delivery method.

USPS

The United States Postal Service (USPS) is, of course, one of the main methods for sending anything. If you are sending a bulk mailing, you will want to check with the post office for the current regulations concerning how the letter needs to be prepared (zip code order, open envelopes, etc.). In an attempt to compete with all the other delivery methods, the USPS now offers many options, from overnight service to delivery confirmation and other tracking methods.

One of the good things about the USPS is that every town has a post office so it can be very convenient.

Couriers

Federal Express (FedEx), United Parcel Service (UPS or "Brown"), as well as several other smaller delivery services such as DHL give you the ability to send a letter overnight with confidence. All of these couriers are expanding their offerings all the time, with FedEx having added two-day and a more economic three- to five-day option.

Your choice of courier may sometimes depend simply on where your letter is headed. You may have already chosen a delivery service to set up an account with because it is the most logical choice for the majority of places to which you send things. You can certainly use any one of the other delivery services for any individual need; you just won't get the good rate that you probably negotiated with the service you set up an account with.

Letters as E-mail Attachments

Sometimes e-mail is the best way to send a letter. But send it as an attachment to the e-mail, not in the body of the e-mail. An attachment is a much more "formal" document and can be printed out void of any introductory e-mail comments; also, the printed document will look just like a letter.

Never, however, send your letter as an attachment without including a note in the main e-mail indicating you are sending an attachment regarding whatever the letter is about. Some office firewalls prohibit attachments from getting through without the sender being included on a list that allows their attachment through computer security. If that isn't the case, sometimes people often automatically trash e-mail attachments without a personal note since viruses are often created that attach themselves to e-mail lists, make it look like the e-mail is from someone you know, and the virus is launched once you open the attachment. So forewarn your recipient that you are sending an e-mail with an attachment by sending an e-mail first without an attachment, telling them to expect one with the attachment to follow.

Fax

Faxing is a good way to send a letter that needs to get to someone right now. However, if your letter needs to look good when it arrives, fax is not the way to do it. Fax letters, on the recipient's end, often look very messy and unattractive. If the letter, however, is just for information purposes and it is more important for it to get there immediately than for it to look pretty, then fax can be the best delivery method. Faxed letters are also good if you need to send a letter immediately that also needs to include something like a magazine article or product literature.

Federal Express and many other delivery services offer not only next-day service but also your choice of whether the next-day delivery happens in the morning (priority overnight) or the afternoon (regular overnight). There are two things to keep in mind about spending the extra money for priority service (you didn't think it was a free choice, did you?):

1. Many times, especially in deliveries to larger cities, the overnight delivery gets delivered in the morning anyway.

2. If you really want morning delivery, you should check to be sure that the recipient's area even gets this service. This is especially true for rural areas and many home deliveries.

   The lesson is that if you want priority overnight service and it is important enough to pay extra, that's great—just make sure you will actually get the service.

CAUTION

Chapter 1

Basic Sales Planning Strategy

If you are beginning to sell because you bought or started a new business, you will most likely have a business plan to help you strategize your selling efforts. Even the most seasoned businesses should have a simple business plan that can help direct sales strategy. Some of the things to include in that strategic plan are:

- Who is your target market? What segment of consumers is your product or service aimed at? Teens? Young adults just leaving college? Young couples on the verge of being first-time homebuyers? Thirty-five-year-old men who are starting to see signs of balding or thirty-five-year-old women who are noticing quite a lot of grey hair? Map out that market from the most general similarities to the most distinguishing details and get a real sense of where your product or service fits in.

- How do you plan to reach them? Hopefully, if you are reading this book, the written word will be part of your plan.

- What kind of language appeals to them? You won't write the same letter to sell to the 60-year-old nurse as you will to the 19-year-old surfer.

- Where will you get your lists of prospects? Target mailing lists ahead of time. Find other ways to get your written message out there—in flyers with complementary companies' products, a letter in the local paper. Be creative and use your resources wisely.

Sales Force

Who is going to help you sell? You may be small enough to be doing all the selling yourself. Or you may be a sales manager in a large corporation with 35 sales reps accountable to you.

Whatever the case, you need to determine how many sales people it will take to cover the territory you need to cover to sell as many products or as much of your service as will help you meet your revenue projections.

Commission Reps

Some sales representatives work for themselves. They may be the sole rep or they may have a group of reps working for them. They will take on your products and will also sell other companies' products. If the other products they sell are complementary to yours, commission groups can be a great way to go. You pay them only for what they sell.

The fact that a commission rep groups sells yours and several other products, all of which appeal to the same target market, can mean your product gets in front of a lot more potential customers than it might on its own. People like to feel they are being efficient in their purchases.

The commission group, as its name implies, works only on commission. You need to supply them with the marketing and sales materials they need to tempt people to buy your product. But you only pay out money to them when they make money for you.

In-House Reps

Some companies have all in-house sales staff. This can be an expensive option—you pay them as employees and typically they also receive standard company benefits. But their base salary can be modest and made up for in commission and bonuses. The good news for them is that their salary can have no upper limits. The bad news for you is that you are paying a base salary to them no matter how little they sell in that period.

Why can house reps be good to have? First, they are selling your product and no one else's. Even though commission reps typically try to sell only complementary lines, you have no control over whose lines they take on. Second, in-house reps become extremely familiar with your company's product or service. While commission reps can also be very familiar with your offering depending on the amount of sales support you provide them, there is still nothing better to get to know a company than to be an employee.

Combination

Some companies have a combination of house reps who sell to the major, national accounts and commission reps who sell to outlying areas of the country where it would be difficult and expensive to have a rep travel to regularly. This can be the best of all worlds. However, the best commission groups often sell to the national accounts in their territory and they will want that business from you as well.

Tele-Reps

Depending on your business and the range of your territory, selling over the phone with scheduled phone sales meetings can be a great way to do business. It is important that you are organized and have sent materials ahead of time for the customer to review so that you can have a productive phone session and they can get any questions they have answered. If they are computerized and you have a good web site, that can be another way to provide information while the sales rep is on the phone with the customer.

Your Message

This is a book about letters, and before you begin writing letters you need to decide what the message is that you are wanting to get across. What can you say to make it clear to the reader that he or she needs your product or service? What is the benefit to them? Don't begin to put a word on paper before you sort this key thing out.

And all of your selling tools should get across the same message. Don't confuse prospects by saying one thing in a letter and when they call up the web site you mentioned, they read something different. Consistency sells.

Alleviate Objections

Think upfront about what objections prospects will bring up. And have answers. Don't let objections surprise you. There isn't a product made that someone won't find something wrong with. Assure your potential customers that you have thought through every angle and you came up with what you are selling with all those things in mind.

Timing

You will need to schedule sales visits, letters, and phone calls with a logical timing. For instance, in the publishing world, calendars for the following year are sold well ahead of time. If you begin the calendar selling process with a letter, that letter will need to reach potential buyers in the spring.

You need to have printed calendars by early in the summer the year before the date on the calendar and they need to ship to the customer not long thereafter. Stores expect to start displaying calendars early in the fall, even in late summer, to get a jump on getting such dated items all sold before the new year hits. It would not be a good sales strategy to try to sell calendars in October.

Plan out the timing of your product sales periods. You will want to have done this for the financial projections for the year anyway—when most of your sales will come in, what times of year most of your manufacturing expenditures will come in, and so forth.

And if you want to have orders in hand before you manufacture your widgets, that will have implications of its own.

Chapter 2

Sales Letter Style

Two kinds of letter style exist: the standard style and your style. Your letters should be a mix of both. You want to make sure to follow the conventions of good business letter writing, including format. And you want your letters to sound like you.

But before you even get to that point, there are some important things to keep in mind as you write letters. These are the good old standard grammar, spelling, and accuracy rules that any letter worth the paper it is written on should follow.

Accuracy

Accuracy in both your facts and your presentation is key to making sure your readers take your letters seriously. While everything should be fact-checked and spell-checked, a few proofreading-type things to check and double check are:

- **Recipient name:** There are few things that turn a reader off more quickly than his or her name spelled wrong. Or being called Mr. when you are a Ms. or being called Mrs. when you are a Ms. or Mr. If you are using a huge mailing list, you are at the mercy of your list provider. However, if you are creating your own mailing list through your business (and if you aren't, you should be!), use every opportunity to double-check the list. If the client comes into or calls your business and you haven't seen them in a while, politely ask if you could take a couple minutes of their time to check the accuracy of their listing in your database.

- **Recipient address:** This is an important one to ask when you have the client on the phone or in front of you. While some things still get to their intended destination despite some astonishing address misspellings, it doesn't say much for your business when the recipient pulls something out of the mailbox addressed to "Dilver Street" instead of "Silver Street." For the ones that come back to you as undeliverable, be sure to update your mailing list as soon as possible, but definitely before you send another mailing of any kind. It may even be worth a special phone call to the customer. Postage is high enough these days to make this a cost-effective thing to do.

- **Headlines:** If your letter or flyer has large-type headlines, check and double-check these. Headlines commonly include typos because we read over them quickly and we read what we expect them to say. This is a glaring way to get noticed negatively from the recipient of your written piece.

- **Boxed material:** The same goes for boxed information as for headlines; double check them yourself and have someone completely unrelated to the project read them as well.

- **Your business name:** Unless the business name is already imprinted on the piece, check it! It is the utmost of sloppiness to spell your own business name wrong. And people will notice!

Then there are the facts. Before you even sit down to write the letter, you will need to gather the facts, figures, statistics, etc. if you plan to use any in your letter. As you do this, keep notes on your sources. If you call people and ask questions to gather information, keep their name, the company they work for, their position at the company, and their contact information on file. If you need to back up your facts or recheck their accuracy, this way you have easy access to where you found them in the first place.

Ditto if you find the information on the Internet or from a book source. Make note of the web site or the name of the book (including author, publisher, ISBN number, and copyright date) and where you found the book so you can get back to it easily.

Grammar

This is where you will wish you paid more attention in those boring high school English classes that focused on grammar. You won't need to diagram any sentences, but if you want to look and sound professional you will do yourself a favor by brushing up on your grammar skills.

You don't need to go it alone however. There are numerous books that can wait patiently by your side and provide all the help you need as you write and rewrite your letters. A few include:

- *The Elements of Style* by William Strunk, Jr., and E.B. White. Known informally as "Strunk & White," this succinct little book on grammar and style issues is well worth the shelf space you give it. While it is not an easy reference book, if you thumb through it you will find all of those grammatical details that have plagued you all of your life—like the difference between affect and effect; the proper use of "few" and "less"; how to form possessives and plurals; and a section on style. While these tips are not targeted specifically to sales letter writing and some of the style tips may be counter to what is considered effective marketing copy, this book is not to be dismissed.

- *Merriam-Webster's Collegiate Dictionary*. The last hard copy as of this writing is the

11th edition. Now that is a moot point, as you can find a Merriam-Webster dictionary online (www.m-w.com) and search words for free. This is the most commonly used dictionary in publishing circles and will do for your needs as well. There are other dictionaries (including others published by Merriam-Webster) that you can also download from a CD to your computer and use when you aren't online or aren't near a server. Don't hesitate to use this incredible tool, either for spelling or for definition confirmation. It only takes a second and it is critical to the credibility of your letters.

- *The Chicago Manual of Style*. This book is almost an institution in itself, the bible of all copyeditors and proofreaders. Although a little confusing in its organization, once you get the hang of it you will be amazed by how you can find almost everything you can imagine regarding grammar and usage in this comprehensive book. Other style manuals exist as well, and any of them might be the one that works best for you. *The Associated Press Style Book* might work, as well as *Words Into Type*. The key is to pick the one that works for you—or the one that is standard for your audience—and be consistent. Customers will notice.

Grammar Pitfalls to Avoid

You don't have to be a grammar genius to write good letters but you do need to avoid the most common grammar pitfalls that make your letters look less than polished. These include:

- Use "among" when comparing several items, "between" when comparing two. For example, "She sat among a group of her peers" and "She sat between two of her peers."
- "Me" is an object, "I" is a subject. For example, "You and I are the only ones dressed in red." "The package came for you and me." A good way to check yourself on this rule is to say the sentence without the "[blank] and" part and see if it sounds right. Using the above examples, "Me am the only one dressed in red" wouldn't sound right, nor would "The package came for I."
- Learn the difference between "affect" and "effect." According to our friend Merriam-Webster, "affect" is a transitive verb and means "to act upon." In fact, another definition is "to produce an effect upon" such as "areas affected by Hurricane Katrina." "Effect" is a noun or a transitive verb. As the former, it is defined as a result or outcome, as in "he began to need more of the medication to get the same effect." As a verb, it is defined "to cause to come into being," e.g., "specific medications effect (meaning "cause") specific diseases."
- Learn how to use apostrophes correctly. The main two uses of apostrophes are for possessives and contractions. Strunk and White give the example of "It's a wise dog that scratches its own fleas." The first "It's" can be read "it is" but the second cannot. If you wonder about an apostrophe for other words, try saying the sentence with the two full words of the contraction. Better yet, use both words instead of the contraction!
- Commas are a common issue with all but the most learned copyeditors. A good rule of thumb is to keep commas to a minimum! That said, always use a comma for a pause or if it makes a sentence more clear.

In Style

You know the overall style of the business you are in. You talk in that style to colleagues over the phone. Use that same language style in your business letters. At the same time, some letters require you to be a little more formal than others. Adjust to fit the situation.

The best way to develop your sales letter-writing style is to get writing! There are, however, some tried-and-true techniques to keep in mind:

- Keep your letters simple. Use short sentences that are clear and concise. Don't use flowery language and big words just to sound smart—you won't sound smart because you will lose your reader before he even gets through the letter. Unless you are writing a letter trying to convince people to take your class on how to write with big words, let those words remain in the dictionary.

- Figure out your target audience and write to them. Women executives will expect different language than male personal trainers. You don't have to get too carried away but you do need to make readers feel the letter was written to them.

- Convey credibility. Use appropriate terms for the industry. Cite sources for any statistics you use. Include quotes from credible business owners or other respected people in the industry (with their permission, of course).

- Be accurate! Check your facts. Have someone else, even more than one person, read your letters before you send them. If you are promising something that will be delivered by another department, check with that department head to be sure you are conveying the right message.

- All that said, get your personality across in your letters! People reading letters like to know that a real person is behind the letter and the only way to get that across is to sound like you. Good sales letters sound personable and convincing.

---

9 Tips to Effective Business Writing

1. Outline what you want to get across in your letter before you start writing.
2. Once you have decided what your main message is, stick to it. People don't have time to read your meanderings; they will just stop reading.
3. Use bulleted and numbered lists to help break up the text and make the letter easier to read. Big blocks of text look daunting to people.
4. Start off lively and to the point. Lively doesn't need to mean cute or silly. But don't bore readers with the first sentence. Pick the most interesting fact about what you are trying to sell and lead with that—and follow it up immediately with why that fact makes this product perfect for the reader to buy.
5. Don't make any promises you can't fulfill—either for goods, services, or turnaround time.
6. Fact check, spell check, and recheck everything.
7. Have someone read your letter. If the letter is a marketing tool, pick someone who is a member of your target audience. Also, have them question facts and spelling while they read.

8. Personally sign the letter if at all possible. If it is a 10,000-letter mailing then of course that is not possible. But if it's just 25, get out your best pen and practice your autograph.
9. Lastly, send the letter to the right audience.

Proofreading Pitfalls to Avoid

- Don't rely on your computer spellcheck! Certainly use it, but consider it the first-round pass. Remember that words that are spelled correctly may still be the wrong word!
- Watch for common misspellings and word choice errors. Some of the most common ones are "they're, their, there"; "accommodate"; and the use of "effect, affect."
- Keep a good dictionary on your bookshelf (and on your computer too if you want). A good thesaurus is also not a bad idea—even the best writers have a block here and there that a synonym finder can help clear.
- Don't use "ain't" and other grammatically incorrect words just to sound casual. In a letter, these things don't sound casual, they sound demeaning to your reader.

Chapter 3

Sales Letter Basics

Letterhead

In short—get some. With the ease of computer software, you don't even need to get any printed—this is especially useful if you are a small business with fewer than a half dozen employees. A color printer allows you to create letters on letterhead as you go.

Word processing programs such as Microsoft Word get more and more sophisticated in what they offer with every new version. You can use their Publisher programs to create a letterhead that you save as a blank to a file; every time you plan to write a letter, call up the "letterhead" file and create your letter on the template.

Most of these programs automatically move the lower part of the letterhead (usually the address area) to the next page and number the pages as you create your letter. Keep a supply of nice stationery on hand and simply print out your letters with the letterhead as you go.

Like anything to do with marketing your business, decide on a color scheme and typeface for your letterhead and stick with it. Likewise for your stationery color. When customers and clients get a letter on grey paper with dark purple letterhead type a few times, they will immediately associate it with your business.

> No matter what color your stationery or the type for your letterhead, type the body of your letters in black. Black ink is cheaper and often comes in bigger cartridges. And it is always easier to read. If you do break this rule once in a while for effect, whatever you do don't print any type in yellow; it is almost always unreadable.

TIP

Format

There is a very simple format to follow for almost any letter. Be sure to use it. If you want to be more casual in the body of the letter that is fine, but keep the letter's appearance formal and neat. It is the best impression to make on all customers you contact by letter.

The chapters in Parts 2 and 3 show many examples of the actual format, but there are basically the following fundamentals to include:

- **The date**, upper left or right side of page. It seems like a no-brainer, but the date is easy to forget to include. You want to make sure recipients of your letters know exactly when it was written. And if someone files a letter away for future reference, it is important for them to be able to know at a glance when the letter was written. Putting the date on the right side allows you to put it on the same line as the recipient's name, which gives you an extra line of space to help keep the letter to one page if necessary. In the examples in this book, we have included it on the upper left side of the page.

- **Recipient's name**, upper left corner in line with or under the date. Use the appropriate salutation. Make sure the person's name is spelled correctly—even the simplest last names can have several alternate spellings. For men, Mr. is always appropriate unless the person is an elected official or holds some office such as Reverend. See the sidebar in this chapter for a list of common prefixes to use in certain instances. In the case of women, always use Ms. unless you know for certain that Miss or Mrs. is correct and preferred.

- **Recipient's address**, upper left corner below name. Be sure you have the correct address for the recipient, that street names and towns are spelled correctly, and that the zip code is correct. First, this is good public relations with the recipient. Second, either a mail merge program or a person addressing envelopes/labels will likely use this address to affix to the front of the envelope—you want to be sure the letter gets to where you want it to go.

- **Sign off**, flush left, one line space after the end of letter: Keep it simple. "Sincerely" is the most common and probably the best sign-off to use especially for letters to people you don't know. Others include "All the Best," "Most Sincerely," and a few variations.

- **Signature space**, 3 to 4 line spaces below sign-off. Leave enough room for you to hand-sign the letter. If you are sending a mass mailing and someone is going to stamp your signature, fine, but you need space for it. However, if you are trying to keep the letter to one page and need a line or two, this is a place to grab it. A hand-signed letter says a lot.

- **Your name**, flush left, below signature space. Type your name no matter how legible your signature is. People want to be sure they have the correct spelling of your name.

- **Your title**, flush left, directly below your name. Type the title you hold at your company. This is one of the most important parts of the business letter—the recipient definitely wants to know from what layer of bureaucracy in your company they are receiving the letter.

The Paperless Office?

When computers started to appear on every desktop in business across the nation (and the world), there was great chatter about the paperless office. Like the Y2K scare and predictions about the end of the printed book, this simply has not come to pass and is unlikely to in any near future. We like paper. We like things to be printed on paper, whatever the reason—it is easier to read, we can make notes on it, paper makes a document seem more real, we don't have to turn something on and wait for it to boot up in order to read a letter. File cabinets will not be obsolete any time soon.

That said, there are some things that can be kept electronically, especially if your office has developed a simple backup system. If your office is big enough, an IT department will be doing backup on your company-wide server on a daily basis. These backups get stored, and while they are not always easy to access for one simple little letter, if something really needs to be tracked down it can be.

On a smaller scale, you can keep a backup of your letters fairly easily. Keep an electronic "folder" that is titled "Letters" and the year. Or if you write a lot of letters, do it by month. At the end of each week (or daily if it makes you feel better) save this file to a jump drive or some other portable storage device. Not only does this give you the backup you want, but you can tote that device with you if you use a laptop outside the office for some of your work.

There are many ways to do this—save the Letters file and e-mail it to your laptop once a week and use that as your backup storage, for example. Choose a system that works for you. And then use it.

And, just like how you will use the letters in this book as templates for your own personalized letter, letters can be recycled time and again. Call up the Letters file, look for a letter that best matches your current need, and change the pertinent information. Then proofread it carefully—you want to be sure you didn't leave any details from the old letter in there that you didn't want!

Chapter 4

Fax/Memo/E-Mail Basics

You will be using all sorts of written forms with which to sell your products and services. Most of this book covers letters, but faxes, memos, and e-mails are all going to be part of your overall written sales campaigns and sales management as well.

Memo Basics

The "memo," short for memorandum (plural "memoranda"), is typically an in-house document. In fact, Merriam-Webster's definition is "a usually brief informal communication typically written for interoffice circulation on paper headed 'memorandum.'" The memo is used to make announcements such as policy changes, new hirings, or promotions; reminders of policy or regulations or an upcoming event; or general information that employees need to know to do their jobs as well as possible.

Memos can be company-wide or intradepartmental. They can also be interdepartmental, depending on whether the information in the memo needs to be exchanged only between two departments.

Format

Memo format is fairly simple. Some companies have stationery or a digital template with MEMORANDUM printed at the top. If so, you can delete the word "memo" from the following format. Otherwise, at the top of the page you need:

- **Memo to** (or just "To:"): Indicating who the memo is directed to. It can be an individual person or it can be a group of employees or the entire company. In sales, a memo will often be addressed to the sales staff.

- **Memo from** (or just "From:"): People reading the memo should be told from whom the information is coming. Be sure to indicate your title and/or department. Unless you are in a very small company, don't assume people know your first and last name.

- **Date:** Always date every written correspondence, even the simplest memo.
- **RE:** This is the reason for the memo. Keep it to a couple words or a short phrase; you don't want the RE: line to be almost as long as the memo itself.
- **Number of pages:** Always indicate how many total pages in length the memo is. If the memo is longer than one page, indicate the page number (1 of 3, 2 of 3, etc.) on each page to make sure recipients know they have received the entire memo.
- **Extenuating information:** Note if the memo is confidential—i.e., the information is not intended to leave the company. That said, keep in mind that memos will easily end up in outside hands, often simply by accident.

The Body of the Memo

Keep memos brief and to the point. It is not necessary to be chatty or conversational. You don't really even have to use complete sentences, although it is always better to do that if space allows for it.

Use normal punctuation and paragraphing in a memo. It does not need to be signed at the bottom in a letter-style signature space, although you may want to put your signature beside your name at the top, especially if the information being put forth in the memo is of the sort that might cause people to question the authenticity of the memo (like announcing a big price reduction).

Accuracy

Like all written correspondence, have someone else read the memo before you send it out to the masses. Be sure to pick someone who is a good proofreader and has good grammatical skills. Accuracy in any correspondence, in-house or not, is an important part of portraying an image of credibility and professionalism.

> If you are the boss or the owner, be sure your written correspondence is as well written and accurate as you expect your employees' correspondence reflecting your company to be.

Fax Basics

The facsimile or "fax" machine, patented by Alexander Bain, a Scottish mechanic, in 1843, was a natural progression from Samuel Morse's telegraph technology. Faxes are signals received through telegraph wires that transmit images onto paper. The fax machine's heyday was the first three-quarters of the twentieth century, before the proliferation of e-mail and electronic ways to scan and transmit images quicker and with higher quality than the fax.

Despite the common use of e-mail, faxes still serve a purpose. Most offices do have a scanner and it isn't that complicated or lengthy of a process to scan images, but it is one more step. With a fax machine, you walk to the machine with your piece of paper, feed it into the machine, dial the number, and press "start." No need to scan the image first. The quality of the image received by the recipient depends greatly not only the quality of the original but on the caliber of machine the image is being printed off at the other end.

Typically faxes are not high enough quality for today's publication standards. They can be just fine for transmitting information as long as the text and image are readable by the recipient. However, if you are trying to impress a potential client with your fine china patterns or the quality of your flooring, a fax of photographs is not going to cut it. Send an overnight package of your high-quality marketing materials to show your products at their best.

Fax Sales

Another area that has become prevalent in the past few years is blanket marketing via the fax. When telemarketing got out of hand and regulations came into play that limited the use of telemarketing and allowed people to sign up to the federal "Do Not Call" list, telemarketers needed to find a new way to market to the masses. Faxes became an option.

The value of trying to sell using this option is questionable. Recipients often get annoyed with the number of unsolicited marketing faxes that come through their machines—the bottom line is that you are using the recipient's fax toner and paper to send your message. And neither of those is cheap. If you have a previous relationship with the client and you know the information is something they will want to know about (a blow-out overstock sale on a product they order regularly), that fax may be welcomed by your customer.

The chances of the fax just getting thrown away unread, or torn in pieces and used for scrap paper, are high. But there is no way for the recipient as yet to stop the unsolicited fax from actually coming in, so if it is a marketing tool that has been used with some success in your industry, you might want to give it a try.

Just the Fax

Faxes should be quite simple. You want to send some information on paper immediately. You write a fax and send it along to the person you want to receive it. The most common faxes are:

- **Very brief.** Typically you are just providing some information to the recipient, which it would be helpful for the recipient to have immediately and in writing.
- **Cover sheets for something else.** The fax memo that you need to create is often just your cover sheet for something else you need to fax, such as a page out of a magazine article, a price sheet, an estimate, or a photo.

The Fax Memo

To create a fax cover sheet (which often comprises the entire fax), you need to include some basic information that you put at the top of the fax. This information is often similar to the information you used to put together a memo and is often in the same style. Include:

- The Recipient's name (TO:)
- Your Name (FROM:)
- The Date (DATE:)
- The Subject of the fax (RE:)
- How many pages the fax is, including the cover sheet (# of pages including this one:)

Always put page numbers on multi-page faxes. If there are many pages, the fax machine on the other end may spit out the pages onto the floor and the recipient will be left trying to figure out the order of the pages. Likewise, as your fax machine sends the multi-page fax, the sheets may end up deposited on the floor, so page numbers may be very helpful to you too.

TIP

When Faxes Are Not Good to Use

When should you not use a fax? Confidential information should rarely if ever be sent via fax machine. Perhaps if you know for sure that the recipient works in a one-person office and you are 100% sure the recipient will be the person picking the fax off the machine, then that is ok. But faxes simply are not private enough to be used to send confidential information.

Material containing photos that are critical to the information also are best not faxed. Even the best faxes are not good photo printers. You would be better to photocopy the material on a high-quality copier and send that or send originals if possible. You can use overnight mail and get the package where it needs to go pretty quickly.

Of course, you can always fax the pages and follow up with the original material if you want the information to get to the recipient quickly but need to have clear photos too.

Basically, anything that requires a high-quality presentation should not be sent via fax machine. The quality on the other end just isn't good enough. Unless the recipient has specifically requested a fax, which means he or she understands that it may not look as nice as it could, then using overnight mail is really your better option.

E-Mail Basics

As e-mail became used more and more it developed a reputation for sloppiness. E-mails were presumed to not fall under the same standards as other written correspondence. They have been considered fast, cryptic messages, especially for those growing up with instant messaging, which by very nature is written in a kind of code.

Don't fall into this trap. Sure, if you are writing chatty messages to your friends and you don't want to take the time to check your spelling, that isn't a big deal. But if you fall into the habit of not checking any e-mail for spelling and grammar, and not caring if you use accurate spellings of names and appropriate punctuation, you will begin to do this with other e-mail messages as well—whether they are to your buddies or not.

Any e-mails used in sales should be carefully crafted and follow all the same basics as any other written correspondence.

E-mail Etiquette

There are some basic etiquette issues specific to e-mail that are important to follow; see below for a few of the most commonly encountered ones. One important issue to understand is that e-mails do not come across the same as a voice on the phone. Any written correspondence has the same potential problem, but e-mail writers often fall into a false sense of connectedness to the person to whom they are writing because e-mails can be almost as immediate as a phone call. But the tone of voice and ability to explain immediately when you sense someone doesn't understand is missing from e-mail. And this can get you in big trouble—especially if you are trying to close a deal, which probably should never be done via e-mail.

Reread e-mails a couple of times before you push the button. Be sure you have not said "can" when you mean "can't" and check for other typos that create crucial changes in meaning. Double-check who you have entered in the "To" line before you hit the Send button—the last thing you want is to reveal to a customer some other customer's sales information. When you pull a name from your address book, it is so easy to put the wrong name in there.

Here are other things to keep in mind:

- Never send confidential information via e-mail. Once you push the send button on your e-mail it is too late to take it back, even if you realize you had the wrong person in the "To" line!

- DON'T USE ALL CAPS. This is considered "shouting" in the e-mail world and is considered offensive.

- If you are responding to one person from an e-mail that was sent out to several people, hit the "reply to sender" button, not the "reply to all" button. It is annoying to have to weed through messages that are a personal conversation between just a couple people.

- Reserve the "high priority" button for things that are, in fact, high priority. Overusing high priority designation is like the old story of the boy who cried wolf—no one will believe you when you send an e-mail that truly is high priority.

- Do not encourage, and certainly do not forward, joke e-mails, chain e-mails, and other e-mail junk mail. Not only does this send the wrong message about your seriousness about your business, but these e-mails are often carrying viruses.

- Don't use obscene language in your e-mails. This is just common courtesy.

- Keep attachments to a minimum. Many companies have software that doesn't allow attachments through the firewall, and so your e-mail may not get through anyway. If you must send an attachment, contact the person ahead of time to make sure they will accept it.

E-mail is a critical part of business correspondence these days. It can save a lot of money on phone calls and employee time that is used with phone calls, since phone calls always entail some chitchat. Training employees to properly use e-mails to represent your company is always in your company's best interest.

E-Mail Policy

All companies should have a policy about e-mails. If you own the company, be sure to create this and alert all employees to it. If you are an employee, be sure you know company policy and adhere to it. E-mail policies can avert lawsuits stemming from everything including accidental virus dispersal to language and discrimination issues. And if you want (or don't want) sales staff to use e-mail, specify what is ok and not ok for it to be used for.

Check and Recheck

When you reread your e-mails, double- and triple-check the name of the person you have chosen from your address book. There are many e-mails you would prefer not to send to the wrong person—although, that said, it is probably a good policy to never put anything in an e-mail you wouldn't want someone else to see. The person you send it to may forward it on without your knowledge or by accident. And if you do send an e-mail to the wrong person, you may never find out that the intended recipient never got the e-mail.

Use the memo format to pass along a single, important piece of information.

Memo Correcting Information

MEMORANDUM

TO: All [STORE NAME] Stores

FROM: Corporate Sales Office

DATE: 18 May 2006

RE: Ad correction

Please be advised that the flyer that is being distributed with the Sunday May 28 papers has incorrect information. The Brand-X grill is listed as being on sale for $149.95. In fact the sale price is $129.95.

Please post the attached correction sheet near the entrance to your store and in the area where you display grills.

We apologize for the inconvenience.

Fax

FAX TO: [recipient]
FROM: [sender's name and title]
DATE: [date]
RE: Overstock sale

# of pages: one

50% OVERSTOCK SALE ON BLACK WIDGETS

Dear Customer:

We are alerting all of our customers who have bought our widgets that we have a current overstock of the black version of this widget. You will want to take advantage of our offer of a 50% discount on these black widgets.

Please note that this sale extends through 31 August, so be sure to place your order before then. This sale is while supplies last.

Always include your phone and e-mail address in e-mail correspondence, especially those involving new business. You don't want someone to have to search for your phone number.

E-mail Responding to Potential Ccontract

TO: Ed Smith

CC: [blank]

SUBJECT: contract

Dear Mr. Smith:

Thank you for thinking of me regarding the [name] project. I thought of a couple more things you could send that would be helpful in estimating how many hours this project might take:

- the previous version of the report
- how many products you think it might include
- whether I should produce the final version and all copies you would need or whether you will print and collate them at your office

Thank you for thinking of me for this project.

Sincerely,

[Name]
[Phone]
[E-mail address]

Part 2

Letters for Prospecting

Chapter 5

Letters of Introduction

Letters of introduction come in many forms. You can introduce

- a new company
- a new product
- a new service
- a special sale
- a new sales person
- a seasonal special

Introduce the Company

If you are sending to your in-house list of current customers, you can assume that the recipient knows you or your company by name. Otherwise, introduce your company briefly, either at the beginning or at the end. Be sure to highlight the reason for your letter so it doesn't get buried. Either put the text in a box or boldface the text or print the sales description in a different color.

You will want to introduce your company as a new owner if you have taken over for another company. Customers tend to be quite loyal and you have to be careful to be positive both about the previous company and about the value of your having taken over the company.

Include a small tri-fold brochure in any mailed piece if at all possible. Take every opportunity to reacquaint the recipient with your company. And if they already know all about you and don't need the brochure, there's a chance they will hand it on to someone else. They may also throw it in the trash, but they definitely can't hand on something they don't have. Don't be stingy with your printed materials. Create them in a cost-effective enough way that you can feel free handing them out.

TIP

Introduce New Products

Always treat the introduction of a new product as a big deal. Send announcements to existing customers, existing vendors, potential customers, and anyone in between. Offer coupons and discounts as a way in for the customer to try something they are not yet familiar with. Point out the product's key features and explain the benefits of the new product. For existing customers, show how the new product fits in with the other things they purchase from your company.

Introduce a New Service

As with a new product, a new service should be announced with great fanfare. Chances are any new service you take on links in nicely with any service you currently offer. Be sure to point these links out. Make special offers on a combination of services. Use the opportunity of offering a new service to entice customers to order services they haven't used before.

Announce a Special Sale

A letter is a great way to announce a special sale to your existing customers or to prospective customers. Again, make the details of the sale immediately noticeable; don't hide your selling point in the body of the letter. Use boldface or colored text to highlight specials, although use them sparingly—use too much and they don't stand out anymore.

Make sales tempting, but you don't need to give the store away. Customers like to think they are getting a deal on something they need and use. Customers have also become keen to "too good to be true" and won't trust your deal if it is too farfetched.

Announce a Seasonal Special

Use letters to remind customers of the upcoming change in season—get your air conditioner reconditioned before summer, have your car's antifreeze and other fluids checked before winter, get your furnace cleaned in the fall before the heating season starts, get a jump on the landscaping season and sign a contract for a landscaping service in the early spring before they are all booked, reserve kennel space for your dog for the holidays before there's no room at the inn. There are hundreds of opportunities to generate a letter for a seasonal reminder. And customers not only take you up on it, they feel like you are watching out for them by reminding them of things that they need to have done.

Announce a New Sales Person or a Promotion

Introducing a new sales person to your customers in the affected region is important to do before the person has to start making appointments. Customers like to hear from "corporate" about personnel changes, especially if the previous person was well liked or if that person did a poor job. Customers want to know how the new person is going to affect their relationship with your company.

Likewise, announcing promotions is a great opportunity to be in touch via letter with your customers. A company that is enthusiastic about their staff is one that most people want to do business with. And promoting people from within says a lot about a company and how much they value good employees.

Take advantage of all of these opportunities to touch base with your customers or to entice potential customers to use your products and services. Don't miss these chances to remind people of your company and get your name in front of them before they need your product or service and run across the name of your competitor.

New Promotion: Homeowner

If you are soliciting business from new customers, put any special offer up front and end the letter by giving a little history on your company.

[Date]

[Name]
[Company]
[Address]
[City, State, Zip]

Dear:

[Company] is pleased to announce a new program for first-time homeowners. Start a new fuel oil account with us and we'll say "welcome" by calculating 50 gallons of heating oil to your first tank fill-up, at no charge.

It's our way of thanking you for bringing your home heating needs to us. This offer is limited to new customers only. We hope you will call our customer service staff and take advantage of this offer.

[Company] has been serving the greater [City] area for [number of years] and has a reputation for reliably servicing our customers no matter what winter brings. We also offer a full cleaning and maintenance service. Having your heating system maintained now, while it's still summer, will save you making that call in the winter cold!

We look forward to serving you.

Sincerely,

[Name]
[Title]

New Promotion: Software Upgrade

[Date]

[Name]
[Company]
[Address]
[City, State, Zip]

Dear:

We're pleased to announce that an upgraded version of our design tool software [Name] is now available. Businesses who have used Version [#] have asked for enhanced database merging capabilities, and our latest version offers all the ease and functionality [Name] users have come to expect, plus added compatibility with a variety of accounting and check printing software.

We are offering this upgrade to users on a current maintenance and support program, at no charge. We'd like to take this opportunity to offer you this same upgrade, for a limited time, if you renew your maintenance and support contract with us.

Details of our maintenance program and the associated costs are included in this packet. Call our technical hotline, today, and increase the power of [Name] for your business applications.

Sincerely,

[Name]
[Title]

If you have support materials, point out only the key points in your letter and include the materials for further explanation.

New Product

[Date]

[Name]
[Company]
[Address]
[City, State, Zip]

Dear:

Businesses routinely back up their data every night, to assure that customer and financial records are accurate and safe. These types of backups are generally performed by someone in the IT Group, and done late in the evening.

What happens, then, to those businesses that are either so small they don't have an IT group, or need to have this critical function automated?

We're excited to announce that we have joined forces with [Company] and can now offer our customers an automated secure backup that uploads to a web portal. The details of this product can be found in the enclosed flyer, and we are offering this product to a select group of existing customers only.

We'd like to show you how it works, in an interactive web demo, taking place on [date and time] at [www.xxx.xxx]. Please fill out the enclosed reservation form, and our technical support staff will send you an installation file that you should run prior to this demonstration.

Space is limited, so please let us know right away if you're interested.

Sincerely,

[Name]
[Title]

If a product can offer safety in any form, mention it right up front in your sales letter. Safety is always a key selling point for any product.

New Product: Existing Customer

[Date]

[Name]
[Company]
[Address]
[City, State, Zip]

Dear:

For the past [number] years, [Company] has provided our clients with the most up-to-date call center technology. Customers who use our "On the Call" agent software know that agents are more focused and spend less time understanding customer needs because their browser opens to the exact page the customer is viewing, when the call begins.

We're pleased to announce a new bolt-on feature of this software, available to customers using Version [#] and later. "Lead Manager" is a server-based module that tracks each agent's call, and by capturing the web pages the agent is led to by customer interest, can provide data and analysis of the most frequently visited areas on your web site.

When used in conjunction with "Call Manager," Lead Manager can give your call center manager a complete picture of each call, to track sales, drop-offs, popular products, and much more.

Please accept the enclosed demo CD and give this new feature a try for 15 days. Instructions for the download are included, but if you have any questions, please call our technical support staff for assistance.

Sincerely,

[Name]
[Title]

Although the featured item for sale doesn't come until the second paragraph in this letter, the first paragraph outlines the key benefits of the product for the customer.

New Product: Existing Customer

Specify when the product will be ready for roll-out. Offering demonstrations for new software can be a selling point for those customers who are a little less than computer-savvy.

[Date]

[Company]
[Address]
[City, State, Zip]

Dear:

[Company] is pleased to announce that we will be offering a new product beginning the 4th quarter of this year. "Get a Grip" will provide HR managers with the ability to track employees' hours and send a complete report to us, for weekly payroll processing.

"Get a Grip" uses the latest in biometrics. Set-up requires that each employee have their thumbprint scanned, and punching in and out is as simple as placing their thumb on the scan pad, and letting the machine "read" their print.

Our sales team will be contacting you in the next few weeks to set up a demonstration. If your company is interested in becoming a beta-test site, please let us know.

We're sure you will find "Get a Grip" a simple and unique way to manage employee time.

Sincerely,

[Name]
[Title]

New Service: Existing Customer

[Date]

[Name]
[Company]
[Address]
[City, State, Zip]

Dear:

For many years, companies in the [Name] industrial park have told us their employees are requesting a more diverse choice of meals than has been available.

We're proud to announce a new service that we think will benefit the employees who spend many hours at their jobs, and will also benefit employers by making sure their staff have healthy, well-balanced choices for meals and snacks.

We have entered into an arrangement with 5 local restaurants that will take turns day-to-day being the "featured meal choice" for the industrial park. Each company will receive the menu of the week, for each participating restaurant, on Monday morning. Employees who want to order from that day's restaurant can give their request to reception by 10:30 a.m., and meals will be delivered between 12:00 and 1:00 p.m.

The details of this program are attached. We hope your employees will find this a healthy alternative to fast food, or an occasional break from the brown bag lunch.

We're interested in your feedback as well, as we want to provide this service as efficiently as possible.

Sincerely,

[Name]
[Title]

If you are responding to consumer requests, be sure to mention it. It is a clear sign that your company is willing to fill a need.

New Service: Existing Customer

[Date]

[Name]
[Company]
[Address]
[City, State, Zip]

Dear:

Thank you for being such a loyal customer. We appreciate your utilizing our lead qualification and telemarketing programs, and we're expanding those programs effective immediately.

In addition to the telemarketing, qualification, and literature mailings you have come to rely on from our agents, we're adding appointment scheduling to our list of services.

Whether you want us to revisit an existing prospect that is now ready to meet with a sales representative, or you want us to assist your outside sales force by preparing sales calls geographically, our trained sales agents are ready to help you.

Your inside sales representative will be contacting you soon, with more details. We hope you'll take advantage of this new service, and the opportunity to add value to each sales call, without adding to your permanent staff.

Sincerely,

[Name]
[Title]

Existing customers love appreciation. Tell them in the beginning of your letter that not only do you appreciate their business, but as a thanks for their business you have something new to sell them that will make their lives better!

New Web Site Announcement 1

[Date]

[Name]
[Company]
[Address]
[City, State, Zip]

Dear:

We're pleased to announce that we have completed the construction of our web site, and we invite you to visit us at [www.ww.com]. We hope you will find it an easy to navigate, and a helpful directory of our products and services, prices, and delivery rates.

Please be sure to visit our feedback page, and let us know what you think!

Sincerely,

[Name]
[Title]

A new or updated web site is a great reason to send a letter announcing the new web site and reminding customers of your business.

New Web Site Announcement 2

[Date]

[Name]
[Company]
[Address]
[City, State, Zip]

Dear:

We've had a tremendous response to our web site for the past several months, and we appreciate your feedback. One of the most commonly requested upgrades to our site was more information on order processes.

We're pleased to announce that you are now able to track the progress of your orders, by visiting a secure password protection portal from our home page. With your order confirmation number, you can check the status of your job, determine an estimated ship date, locate tracking, and download copies of your invoices in a PDF format.

Please continue to provide us with valuable feedback, so that we can enhance our services to you.

Sincerely,

[Name]
[Title]

This is another letter showing the value of letting customers know you are willing to respond to their feedback. There is no better market research than that from your customers.

New Strategic Company Relationship 1

[Date]

[Name]
[Company]
[Address]
[City, State, Zip]

Dear:

[Company] is a worldwide manufacturer and marketer of [Product], and we are pleased to announce that we will now provide them with the packaging materials for their domestic and international shipments.

Representatives from [Company] will be visiting our manufacturing and distribution locations during the week of [date]. Please extend every courtesy to this important customer.

Sincerely,

[Name]
[Title]

This letter could also be an in-house memo or sent to the warehouse and manufacturing plant as a fax—whatever way can provide a written piece to post on bulletin boards and other places where all employees will see it.

New Strategic Company Relationship 2

[Date]

[Name]
[Company]
[Address]
[City, State, Zip]

Dear:

We will be hosting several representatives from [Company], a leading electronics exporter in Taiwan, during [dates]. This organization is one of the premier exporters of the cables and quick disconnects used in our "I hear you" line of headsets. We hope to use this visit to finalize a strategic partnership that has been under discussion for months.

We would like to extend an invitation to all of our employees to join us for a reception on [date] at [Location]. We expect that this relationship will be a large component of our expansion efforts and it is important to [Name] to meet our staff.

Please let your manager know if you are attending, or see him/her with any questions.

Sincerely,

[Name]
[Title]

This is a letter that could be sent to company employees as an attachment to an e-mail rather than printed as a letter and put in everyone's mailbox. However, remember that an e-mail has a lot more chance of being sent accidentally to people you would rather not have see it.

Introductory Letter: New Company 1

[Date]

[Name]
[Company]
[Address]
[City, State, Zip]

Dear:

[Company] is coming to your area! The premier provider of [Product], which has been only available by catalog, will open its first retail store at [Location].

Our opening is scheduled to take place on [date]. Look for more information in the coming weeks, as well as sales flyers in your local newspaper.

We are delighted to be able to offer our product in your community, and look forward to seeing you in the store.

Sincerely,

[Name]
[Title]

Even though the store isn't open yet, it is a great idea to send out advance information to get "the buzz" started about the new store. By the time it opens, people will be waiting in line to get in!

Introductory Letter: New Company 2

Most customers are wary of change, especially companiess being taken over. This kind of upbeat letter with the key benefits up-front can really help a customer find the change positive rather than negative.

[Date]

[Name]
[Company]
[Address]
[City, State, Zip]

Dear:

You've been hearing for months that a change was coming, you've seen the advertisements, and you've heard the radio announcements.

We're [Company], and we're proud to be your new cable and Internet service provider. In the coming months you'll see changes to your billing; these changes will make it easier for you to better understand how you are paying for the service you have. You'll see changes in your channel lineup, as we add new channels, and change the programming so that it is consistent with the cable television channel lineup in the surrounding towns.

One thing won't change, and that's the 24-hour-a-day, 365-day-a-year customer service and technical support availability. If you have questions about your account, want to change your package, or just want to find out more about your new provider, call us.

We look forward to serving your community.

Sincerely,

[Name]
[Title]

Introductory Letter: New Company 3

[Date]

[Name]
[Company]
[Address]
[City, State, Zip]

Dear:

We're proud to announce that the Grand Opening of our flagship store, [Name], will take place on [date]. We're located in the building formerly owned by [Company], and we've taken that wonderful old building, shined her up, and made her look like new again!

The staff of [Company] look forward to seeing you! We hope you will use the enclosed 10% off coupon during our Grand Opening Celebration.

Sincerely,

[Name]
[Title]

If you want to lure a customer to your store, whether it's a new or existing customer or a new or old store, include a discount coupon!

Introductory Letter: New Company 4

[Date]

[Name]
[Company]
[Address]
[City, State, Zip]

Dear:

[Company] has been chosen by the Industrial Park owners as the new food service provider. We'll be taking over the cafeteria space previously occupied by [Company].

Our intent is to open for business during the month of [Month]. We'll be offering a breakfast bar, breakfast grill specials, and lunch specials as well as salad, pizza, and "to-go" specials.

We're having an open house for the management of all companies in the park, on [date and time]. We hope you will join us for complimentary appetizers and beverages. We'd like to meet each of you and learn about your company's schedule, and any special requests you may have had from your employees.

We will also be offering a full catering service, and look forward to providing casual and creative snacks, and meals, for company functions and meetings.

Please let us know if you can join us on [date].

Sincerely,

[Name]
[Title]

A great way to win over customers is to invite them to try what you are offering!

Introductory Letter: New Company 5

[Date]

[Name]
[Company]
[Address]
[City, State, Zip]

Dear:

[Company], a full-service graphic design and consulting business, is open and ready to help your company tell its story.

We are fully staffed with professionals from graphic design, advertising and marketing, and web development backgrounds. Whether you are looking for some short-term help for a marketing survey, or a full-scale consulting team to help you update your image, [Company] can help you.

A brochure with some of our recent accomplishments, industry awards, and upcoming events is included for your convenience. Please contact us for a no-cost, no-obligation consultation. We look forward to helping you refine and deliver your message.

Sincerely,

[Name]
[Title]

Something like a graphic design firm has to have an appealing selling piece. Always include some samples too.

Introductory Letter: New Sales Rep 1

[Date]

[Name]
[Company]
[Address]
[City, State, Zip]

Dear:

It is with pleasure that [Company] announces that [Name] has accepted a sales position with us. [Name] comes to us with many years experience in our industry, most recently with [Company].

[Name] will be responsible for our customers in the following areas: [specify]. [He/She] will be contacting you in the next few weeks to set up an introductory meeting.

I'm sure you will find [Name] knowledgeable about our products and industry, and that you will see no change in the fine service we have provided you over the years.

Please let me know if you have any questions. We value your business and are here to help.

Sincerely,

[Name]
[Title]

New salespeople should always be introduced with a letter before they actually pick up the phone to arrange a sales appointment with existing customers in their territory.

Introductory Letter: New Sales Rep 2

[Date]

[Name]
[Company]
[Address]
[City, State, Zip]

Dear:

For more than [number] years, [Name] has provided you with sales and service for all your [product] needs. Recently, [Name] announced his/her retirement, and after careful consideration of a number of qualified applicants, we are pleased to announce that we have chosen [Name] to succeed [Name], as your Account Representative.

[new rep Name] will contact you in the next few weeks and set up a meeting. During the next 3 months, [he/she] will be meeting all our valued customers with [retiring rep Name] so that the transition will be seamless to you.

We're sure you join us in wishing [Name] a happy, healthy, and busy retirement! We are confident that you will continue to have the same quality service from [Name].

Sincerely,

[Name]
[Title]

Having a reason like a rep retiring is a good reason to announce a new sales rep and should be done at the same time.

Introductory Letter: New Sales Rep 3

Keeping your customers apprised of any changes in sales force is a good way of letting them know that you appreciate them and that you remember that they are the key to your business.

[Date]

[Name]
[Company]
[Address]
[City, State, Zip]

Dear:

Our company continues to grow, and in order to meet our growth, and customer demand for our products, we are pleased to announce that [Name] has been promoted to our Sales Division, effective immediately.

[Name] has been in our telesales division for the past 3 years, and is well versed in our product line. As an inside sales rep for our [Product] division, [Name] will be responsible for managing your inventory, working with you on reorders, and introducing new products as they become available.

You can reach [Name] at [number and e-mail address]. [He/She] will be calling you to introduce [himself/herself] personally.

As always, don't hesitate to contact me, or any member of our Management Team, if we can be of assistance. Thank you for your continued support of our products.

Sincerely,

[Name]
[Title]

Introductory Letter: New Sales Rep 4

[Date]

[Name]
[Company]
[Address]
[City, State, Zip]

Dear:

The President and Management Team of [Company] are pleased to announce that [Name] will take over as Sales Representative for the [Region/Territory], effective [date].

[Name] is a seasoned sales veteran who has come out of retirement to take on this challenging opportunity, and will join us at our National Sales Meeting on [dates].

Please take a moment to introduce yourself at the meeting, and welcome [Name] to our sales team.

The first 6 months of the year have been our best yet, and we have even higher expectations for the rest of this year!

Congratulations on a job well done so far, and welcome, [Name]!

Sincerely,

[Name]
[Title]

This in-house letter announces that reps can expect to see a new face around the table at the next sales meeting. It's best not to surprise employees with new co-workers; it can be looked at as very threatening. Let them help you welcome a new employee.

Introductory Letter: New Sales Rep 5

This letter combines the announcement of a new sales rep as well as the opening of a new store and a promotional giveaway. This is about as many things as you would want to include in a letter. If things can wait, send information about one thing one month, and another thing the next month, giving you reason to keep your name in front of your existing and prospective customers.

[Date]

[Name]
[Company]
[Address]
[City, State, Zip]

Dear:

[Name] has joined [Company] and will be the showroom sales representative for our new retail facility in [City].

Prior to joining our organization, [Name] worked for the past [number] years as a District Sales Representative for [Company], a leading supplier of [product/service].

Our [City] retail store is scheduled to open on [date], and we invite you to stop by, see our full range of [products] for your home, and meet [Name]. We'll have plenty of give-aways, and a grand prizewinner will receive a gift certificate, valued at $1,000 in store merchandise.

Join us, and welcome [Name] to our team.

Sincerely,

[Name]
[Title]

Introductory Letter: Self-Introduction 1

[Date]

 [Name]
[Company]
[Address]
[City, State, Zip]

Dear:

As the new area sales representative for [Company], I'd like to take a moment and introduce myself to you. Although I am new to your region, I've been with [Company] for [number] years. In addition to my sales experience, I am also a factory-trained service advisor.

I will be in your area during [timeframe] and would like to stop by to introduce myself in person. My card with all contact information is enclosed. I look forward to working with you.

Sincerely,

[Name]
[Title]

Always, always include your business card with your written correspondence. Recipients will most likely stick the card in the Rolodex—and who knows, when they are flipping through looking for a vendor, perhaps they'll see your card and give you a try!

Introductory Letter: Self-Introduction 2

[Date]

[Name]
[Company]
[Address]
[City, State, Zip]

Dear:

My name is [Name] and I'd like to stop by your business next week and introduce myself. [Name], as you know, has retired and is spending some well-deserved time traveling and indulging in his love of golf. I have taken over his territory, and am pleased to have this opportunity to work with you. I am proud to carry on the tradition of personal sales and service, the hallmarks of [Company].

I hope you can find a few minutes in your schedule to speak with me, so that I can better understand your business and how [Company] can continue to meet your needs, and exceed your expectations. I look forward to working with you.

Sincerely,

[Name]
[Title]

Reminding customers of their previous rep with whom they had a good rapport will give you an leg up in developing a good initial rapport with them too.

Introductory Letter: Self-Introduction 3

[Date]

[Name]
[Company]
[Address]
[City, State, Zip]

Dear:

I have joined [Company] as their Sales Representative, effective the first of the month. I have had the pleasure of working with many of you in my previous position, as Customer Service Manager, and I hope to combine my service and sales experience to bring you full service support for all your product needs.

I will be in your area on [date] and would like to stop by and say hello. I'll give you a call next week to confirm a time, but please don't hesitate to contact me right away, if I can be of service.

Sincerely,

[Name]
[Title]

Always let people know if you have worked with the company before or whether this is a promotion. First, it says good things about a company that people stay with them and that they promote well-performing employees. Second, it may remind them of having worked with you before.

Introductory Letter: Self-Introduction 4

Get in touch with new clients as soon as possible. Give them a chance to organize their desks, but soon after, get your name in front of them.

[Date]

[Name]
[Company]
[Address]
[City, State, Zip]

Dear:

I spoke with [Name] last week and [he/she] told me that you have relocated to the [City] office. I thought I would write you a short note to introduce myself as your Sales Representative.

I know that you are familiar with our company and products from your prior relationship with us in [former City]. I'd like to call on you as soon as you are settled, so that I can go over the products and ordering cycle your predecessor used with us, and set up a plan that will work for you in the days and months ahead.

If I can do anything to help you acclimate yourself to the area, please give me a call! Congratulations on your new assignment. I look forward to meeting you.

Sincerely,

[Name]
[Title]

Introductory Letter: Self-Introduction 5

[Date]

[Name]
[Company]
[Address]
[City, State, Zip]

Dear:

My name is [Name], and I am the branch manager of the [Bank name]. I'd like to welcome you to our community! My staff and I are here to do anything we can to make your relocation to [City] a smooth transition.

[Bank name] is a full-service facility, with branches at all the malls in the area. I hope you will stop by and give me the opportunity to introduce myself in person. We'd like to be your bank!

Sincerely,

[Name]
[Title]

If you think a customer might bring in enough business to warrant a personal visit, by all means arrange it.

External Policy Change 1

Holiday giving time is always an opportunity to put your company's name in front of your customers in a good light.

[Date]

[Name]
[Company]
[Address]
[City, State, Zip]

Dear:

We'd like to take this time to thank all our valued customers for their business, and we look forward to continuing to do business with you in the years to come.

We are making a change in the way we handle Christmas giving. Beginning with the [year] holiday season, we will make a donation to a charitable organization, on behalf of our customers. Each year, a team of employees will meet and decide which organization we will select, and that information will be included in our company Christmas card.

We hope you will find our new policy one that both shows our appreciation for you, and our desire to help those less fortunate.

Happy Holidays from all of us at [Company].

Sincerely,

[Name]
[Title]

External Policy Change 2

[Date]

[Name]
[Company]
[Address]
[City, State, Zip]

Dear:

We'd like to thank all our vendors for the wonderful support you have given us during this time. We appreciate the many expressions of sorrow you have given us, after the loss of our employees.

In order to give our employees privacy, we are immediately curtailing all vendor visits. We would ask that you honor our wishes and understand that we need to put the physical, mental, and emotional well-being of our staff first and foremost.

We will be available by telephone and e-mail, but will not be open for vendor visits until further notice. We appreciate your understanding.

Sincerely,

[Name]
[Title]

Policy changes during times of crisis should be dealt with quickly. No one wants to be embarrassed, including the people outside the company that have to interact with the company after a crisis.

External Policy Change 3

[Date]

[Name]
[Company]
[Address]
[City, State, Zip]

Dear:

Current events have caused us to examine our security, and we will be changing our policies so that vendors and customers are only allowed in certain areas of the buildings, and then only with the proper identification and escort.

Your cooperation in abiding by these new policies is appreciated.

Sincerely,

[Name]
[Title]

New rules need to be handed out as quickly as they are decided and before awkward circumstances make customers feel unkindly toward your company.

Chapter 6

Letters to Prospects

The key to sending letters to prospects is having prospects! Thinking about potential new customers should be a never-ending process. Prospects are everywhere—sitting beside you on a plane flight, at a cocktail party, in your booth at a trade show, at the hairdresser's.

Turning prospects into customers is more easily accomplished if you really believe in the product you are selling. Some "natural-born" salespeople enjoy selling anything, whether they believe in it or not. But most of us need to feel that the product we are selling not only has some value to potential customers, but that the benefits we are espousing are in fact beneficial, and not just good marketing copy.

Prospects vs. Existing Customers

How you handle prospects is definitely a bit different from how you handle sales to existing customers. While you do need to keep building trust with existing customers, gaining that trust to begin with is the key with prospective customers.

Use your sales letters to start to build that trust. Letters can allow you to spend the time you need to explain your product or service, point out the benefits to the potential customer, and otherwise develop the marketing strategy you need to pull in that particular customer.

Serendipity

Keep marketing materials on you at all times. When you run across those prospects on a flight to Phoenix or at the hairdresser, you can give them a simple brochure with a business card attached to it. Always leave potential prospects with something to remember you with.

And always get their name and address or e-mail address and send a follow-up letter. Remind them, of course, where you met and how the conversation turned to your product— which very well might have been because of some need you recognized in something they said.

For example, maybe you sell all-natural swimming pool cleaning supplies and during your conversation about how the prospect gets through the hot summers in Phoenix, he or she mentioned having a swimming pool in the backyard.

Direct Mail Lists

If you take the time to generate a good sales letter, you want to have some people to send it to. All sorts of list brokers exist from whom you can buy mailing lists. These are the next best thing to the list you generate yourself from your personal prospecting. The more targeted the list and the more reliable the list source, the more it will cost. You can often buy membership lists from organizations, sometimes with a discount if you are a member.

Be sure to go to reputable sources. There is nothing more discouraging than spending a lot of money on brochures, and printing up letters, envelopes, and postage to have a large percentage of the mailing come back to you.

Your Own List

There is nothing more reliable than the mailing list you create yourself. By design, this is probably a list that consists of people who have expressed interest in your company/product already. A good portion of them are probably already customers of yours; always be sure existing customers are on your list to mail a notice about a special to.

Using Existing Customers to Prospect

Your existing customers are among the best sources of prospects who turn into customers. Always offer them an incentive to send friends and family your way—a free gift or a discount coupon on their next visit, for example. They will at least try. And remind them of this offer once a year. Use a simple postcard that doesn't cost much to send and doesn't require they spend much time to read. If you offer a service or product that they need regularly, time the postcard to go out just after they have used your service or bought your product.

Mix It Up

Of course, you will use all of these methods to generate leads for potential sales. The key to increasing sales is to increase your prospects. That's not to say you should simply throw mud at the wall and see what sticks. From all of these different sources, you need to concentrate on what are referred to as "qualified leads"—leads that have a reason to potentially be successful.

Tailor Your Letters

You don't need to make every letter to every potential lead different. But you do need to tailor your letter differently to each different prospect type. The list you buy from the American

Automobile Association is going to require a little different wording than the list you generate from local real estate transactions.

A Plan

Finally, have a plan. Create a strategy for sending letters. Estimate the percentage return you might get from any given list (2-5% is pretty good!) and fit that into your revenue projections. Giving yourself targets gives you concrete goals to aim for. Sales becomes like putting together an interesting puzzle. Then work your letter-writing campaign into your plans.

Prospecting: Bank

One way to find out who has moved to the area is by reviewing real estate trans-actions.

[Date]

[Name]
[Company]
[Address]
[City, State, Zip]

Dear:

Welcome to [City]! We're glad you've chosen to relocate to [City] and hope that you are enjoying your first days as a member of our community.

[Bank] has been providing residents with personal banking services since [year]. In addition to the traditional checking, savings, and loan programs, we also offer CDs at very competitive rates, and for the young homeowner like you, we have a very diverse money market program.

We hope you will stop by, meet our friendly and knowledgeable staff, and feel, as we do, that our bank is "the best bank" to meet your financial needs.

Sincerely,

[Name]
[Title]

Prospecting: Service

[Date]

[Name]
[Company]
[Address]
[City, State, Zip]

Dear:

We'd like to take this opportunity to introduce ourselves as the new owners of [Company]. For the past [number] years, this company has provided the community with full home maintenance services, from outside grounds maintenance to seasonal heavy cleaning.

Although the company itself has changed hands, rest assured that we plan to continue the traditions started by the [Name] family. We hope you will continue to come to [Company] for all your home cleaning service needs. As a special introductory offer, we hope you will take advantage of the enclosed coupon, for 10% off on gutter cleaning and inspection.

We're here to help, and look forward to your call.

Sincerely,

[Name]
[Title]

Customers tend to be loyal. You will want to be proactive with existing customers of a new business you purchase. Be positive about the former owners while assuring them that you not only plan to carry on the good work of the previous owners but things will be even better. And offer a discount to encourage them to stay with you, not change to the other maintenance company in town.

Prospecting: Health Care

New employees are always a reason to send an information letter out to clients. Adding hours is another key benefit that customers will want to know about. Maybe they haven't been using your services much because your hours conflict with their schedule, but now that you are open until 8 on Thursday, they can.

[Date]

[Name]
[Company]
[Address]
[City, State, Zip]

Dear:

We're growing! In response to the tremendous "growth spurt" in our community, we're adding to our health care staff.

Please welcome [Name], a full time family practitioner, and [Name], a licensed nurse/midwife to our family of health care professionals.

[Name] and [Name] are now accepting new patients, and to accommodate the request of our patients we will be expanding our hours to include evening hours by appointment, on Tuesdays and Thursdays until 8:00 p.m., and the second and fourth Saturday of each month, from 9:00 a.m. to noon, again by appointment only.

Stop by and meet the newest members of our team!

Sincerely,

[Name]
[Title]

Prospecting: Auto

[Date]

[Name]
[Company]
[Address]
[City, State, Zip]

Dear:

Our region has been experiencing unprecedented weather for the past 6 months. Extreme cold, high winds, hail, and even flooding have caused damage to many of our homes and businesses.

Our dealership has not been spared, and the recent severe weather damaged every one of the 300 new cars on our lot.

We've decided to, for a limited time only, offer "one hail of a sale."

Residents of this county who can show proof of residency will be able to purchase any new car on our lot, for 10% over dealer cost. This opportunity is subject to credit approval. A number of financing options are available.

We've included a listing of cars and small trucks that are included in this program. Don't wait! Drive, paddle, windsurf your way over to our [City] lot, and hail one of our associates! They're ready to deal!

Sincerely,

[Name]
[Title]

Turn misfortune to your advantage and use it to gain sales and maybe some new customers.

Prospecting: Cable

[Date]

[Name]
[Company]
[Address]
[City, State, Zip]

Dear:

The past year has been one of change for your local cable provider, as they worked to satisfy their obligations to creditors while keeping your cable and Internet service up and running.

We're pleased to announce that we have reached an agreement with [Company], and effective [date] your cable and Internet provider plans will be integrated with our existing programs in the surrounding communities.

In the coming months, you will see changes in your channel lineup so that your cable service is the same as that in [City]. We're proud to be the media supplier to your community, and as an introductory offer, you can now add a movie channel, or other premium service with the first month free.

We hope that this special offer will entice you to check out our full line of available programming. Please contact us if you have any questions regarding your existing, or potential services.

Sincerely,

[Name]
[Title]

Your company can seem like a hero to customers whose provider has been experiencing financial difficulty. Be careful not to be negative about the old company.

Prospecting: Health Club

[Date]

[Name]
[Company]
[Address]
[City, State, Zip]

Dear:

[Name] Health Club has begun a new family membership program, and we'd like to invite you to join! Beginning in [Month] we will offer a full membership program to parents and children. Our facilities offer state-of-the-art exercise equipment, trained fitness and nutrition instructors, an Olympic size swimming pool, and much more!

Please join us at our open house on [date and time] and bring the whole family. Guided tours will take place every quarter hour, and child care for small children (under 5) will be available in the lounge.

It's time to get fit! See you soon!

Sincerely,

[Name]
[Title]

Always be thinking of new programs you can create to entice new members/customers.

Prospecting: Community Center

[Date]

[Name]
[Company]
[Address]
[City, State, Zip]

Dear:

Don't give up too quickly on potential customers. For something like classes, it can take people several seasons of brochures before their schedule allows them to sign on.

We're proud to announce that fall adult education programs will begin on [date]. In addition to the adult GED program, we are now offering 6-week courses for the hobby/enthusiast.

The enclosed brochure outlines the courses, schedules, and fees. Want to learn to make a gourmet meal? Take the cooking class! Interested in stargazing and photography? We have both, for beginner and intermediate students.

Join us, improve your mind, meet new people, and learn a new skill. Registration is filling up fast, so don't delay, give us a call today!

See you at your Community Center—your neighbors and friends are waiting for you!

Sincerely,

[Name]
[Title]

Prospecting: Marina

[Date]

[Name]
[Company]
[Address]
[City, State, Zip]

Dear:

The summer season is winding down, and it's time to start thinking about winterizing your boat or recreational vehicle. Routine maintenance and care of your seasonal equipment will keep it in top condition, ready to go again in the spring!

Stop by today and check out our new boat storage buildings. We can winterize your boat and store it in our heated and weatherproof building. We'll even get it ready and launch it for you!

Check out the enclosed rate card, and call us, if you have a need not listed, for a custom quote.

Put this letter and rate card where you can find it—and go enjoy the last few weekends on the lake!

Sincerely,

[Name]
[Title]

If you have a set rate card, enclose it. If your rates are reasonable and competitive, it will more likely encourage customers than turn them away.

Prospecting: Heating

[Date]

[Name]
[Company]
[Address]
[City, State, Zip]

Dear:

[Company] has been the premier provider of fireplace inserts and combination coal and wood stoves for the past [number] years. We're proud to announce that we are now carrying [Name] Pellet Stoves, the fastest growing type of home heating system.

Pellet stoves burn clean, have low dust and ash content, and require minimum maintenance. Because they don't burn as hot as traditional wood or coal stoves, installation options are more flexible, especially in small or modular homes. Pellets are less costly than wood or coal, and because pellet stoves automatically feed, depending on the setting, heat output does not fluctuate, which maintains the temperature in your home for a more efficient heat.

If you are considering adding to your home heating options, why not consider a pellet stove for comfort, convenience, and safety? We'll be at the [Name] fair during [dates] and will have a variety of models to choose from.

Stop by our exhibit, and see what a difference you can make in your heating cost and comfort by using a pellet stove.

Sincerely,

[Name]
[Title]

This letter does a great job of outlining all the benefits of a product many people may not know much about.

Prospecting: Restaurant

[Date]

[Name]
[Company]
[Address]
[City, State, Zip]

Dear:

[Restaurant] is proud to announce their grand opening on [date]. Your hosts [Names] invite you to join your friends in our lounge for a variety of spirits and light appetizers. Diners of a more adventurous nature will want to try the "mystery meal," 7 courses that will change from week to week. (Advance reservations required).

Whether it's a light lunch, a Sunday brunch, or a meal to commemorate an event, our chef, servers, and staff are waiting to greet you. To celebrate our opening, please join us on [date] for a complimentary cocktail and appetizer, and listen to light jazz performed by [Name].

We look forward to seeing you!

Sincerely,

[Name]
[Title]

For businesses like a restaurant, one way to get customers in the door is to offer them free food and beverages. If they like what they see, eat, and drink, they will definitely be back.

Cold Call Letter 1

Using terms like "bonded staff" is a quick way to indicate to prospects that you are reliable and reputable. They may not know what "bonded" means, which might mean they are curious enough to give you a call to find out!

[Date]

[Name]
[Company]
[Address]
[City, State, Zip]

Dear:

The winter season is approaching, and it's time to start thinking about winterizing your seasonal home. [Company] has been providing winterization services to Lake [Name] residents for over 35 years.

Our bonded staff will come to your camp, drain water pipes, clean and install storm windows and shutters, install window kits; whatever your need is, we can handle it.

Call us today, and get a quote. Let us take care of those "end of season" details, while you enjoy the waning days of summer on Lake [Name].

Sincerely,

[Name]
[Title]

Cold Call Letter 2

[Date]

[Name]
[Company]
[Address]
[City, State, Zip]

Dear:

Today companies are keeping more detailed records of order transactions. Purchase orders, sales orders, vendor acknowledgements, and other data are critical to business records but take up a tremendous amount of space.

[Product Name] will revolutionize your data capture. By working directly with your networked printer, orders and other documents will be scanned, and uploaded to an archive file. Users can review records, print documentation, and e-mail records with the touch of a button.

We'll be in booth [number] at the upcoming [Show name]. Please stop by and see a demonstration of our product.

We don't think there will ever be a "paperless society" but we do think there are some documents that should be seen, but not printed!

Sincerely,

[Name]
[Title]

Trade shows are expensive to attend. Be sure to increase your odds of selling product at a trade show by mailing information to prospects who might be there.

Cold Call: Casual Acquaintance

[Date]

[Name]
[Company]
[Address]
[City, State, Zip]

Dear:

I enjoyed speaking with you last week on the [Airline] flight to [City]. I've given some thought to our discussion about tracking and identifying common customer complaints, and I think our product, [Name], might be what you are looking for.

I've taken the liberty of enclosing some information about [Product] for your review. I'll be back in [City] during the week of [dates] and I'm hoping that you will have some time for a demonstration of our software.

I look forward to speaking with you again soon.

Sincerely,

[Name]
[Title]

Follow up on serendipitous prospects like this one from a flight.

Casual Cold Call

[Date]

[Name]
[Company]
[Address]
[City, State, Zip]

Dear:

I had the pleasure of attending the seminar, [Name], last week, and I was interested in the comments you made during the open discussion about increasing your return rate from Marketing "e-mail blasts."

I am the area sales representative for [Company] and I think that our product [Product] might be the solution you're looking for.

Our product will help you create an eye-catching message, through one of the 300 templates that will get you started creating your message. [Product name] is compatible with most of today's e-mail programs, so once you have drafted your e-mail, it's a simple 2-step process to import your recipient file, and send.

[Product] has a built-in "name scrubber" so that e-mail addresses that are incomplete or formatted incorrectly are noted before the mailing is sent.

I'd love to tell you more about [Product]. I will be in [City] next week, and I hope you will have a few minutes to take my call.

Sincerely,

[Name]
[Title]

Consider everything you do as a place for potential customers. And follow up with a "cold call" letter that introduces you and your product or service to the prospect.

Renewing Contact with Old Prospects 1

[Date]

[Name]
[Company]
[Address]
[City, State, Zip]

Dear:

Last year you had contacted our company and were interested in a distribution agreement for the Southeast. You may recall at that time we were not accepting new distributors for that region. Our sales have increased by 150%, and our current distribution channel is not staffed to handle all the leads in a timely manner, so we are now exploring a second distribution net for the Southeast.

I'd like to talk with you about this opportunity in more detail, if you're still interested. You would receive leads in a 50/50 split with our existing channel partner, competitive distribution pricing, and support from our sales, marketing, and technical support staff.

I'll give you a call next week to discuss. I look forward to exploring this opportunity with you and your team.

Sincerely,

[Name]
[Title]

"Old prospects never die." Keep tabs on people who contacted you but never ultimately did business. Don't pester them, but an annual reminder letter can quite possibly turn into a sale within 3-5 years.

Renewing Contact with Old Prospects 2

[Date]

[Name]
[Company]
[Address]
[City, State, Zip]

Dear:

I'm not sure if you will remember me, as we met 3 years ago at the [Name] show. At that time I was working with [Company] and you visited our booth in Dallas.

I have started my own business working with manufacturing companies that are automating their production equipment. I'd like to call on you next month when I am in Austin, and show you some of the equipment manufacturers I am representing.

I look forward to speaking with you again.

Sincerely,

[Name]
[Title]

When you change jobs or start a new business, send a note to any prior contacts you had. Don't steal your previous employer's customers! But if you are in a different business but some prospects/customers could overlap, contact them—ask your previous employer first if you feel you will be stepping on toes. Besides, a couple of customers is not worth a lawsuit.

Trade Show Prospects 1

[Date]

[Name]
[Company]
[Address]
[City, State, Zip]

Dear:

Thank you for visiting our booth at the [Name] show in Chicago last month. I appreciate your taking the time to discuss our product with you, and hope that I answered all your questions.

Enclosed you will find the additional information you requested regarding modular storage units for heavy equipment. There are buildings like the one you are interested in, set up in our Dearborn facility, and I invite you to visit us when you are in the area.

I will give you a call next week to go over the information. Don't hesitate to call me anytime if you have questions.

Sincerely,

[Name]
[Title]

Again, use your trade show booth to the utmost advantage. Send letters beforehand inviting prospects and current customers to your booth. And follow up after with letters and marketing materials to anyone who stopped by and was at all inquisitive.

Trade Show Prospects 2

[Date]

[Name]
[Company]
[Address]
[City, State, Zip]

Dear:

Congratulations! Your business card was drawn as the winner of our [Name] trade show contest. We appreciate your visiting our booth at the show, and hope you enjoy the enclosed gift certificate, good for dinner for two at [Restaurant].

The product information you requested at the show is also included, for your convenience. Enjoy your night out, and remember [Company] for all your plumbing needs.

Sincerely,

[Name]
[Title]

Using raffles at trade shows (and in your store/ office if you have one) is an excellent way to build your own mailing list.

Prospect Referral 1

[Date]

[Name]
[Company]
[Address]
[City, State, Zip]

Dear:

I was given your name and contact information by [Referral], who mentioned you were looking for a new source for printers and toner.

[Company] has been in business since [year] and is one of the major suppliers of printers and toner to the call center industry. We offer the full line of Lexmark, HP, and Xerox printers as well as toner, accessories, parts, and information on our same-day and next-day on-site service.

The enclosed line card lists the current models of HP printers that are due to be phased out in the fall of 2006. If you are currently using these printers and want to continue to have them serviced and supported, I hope you will consider coming to us.

I will give you a call in at the end of the week to discuss your needs. I look forward to speaking with you.

Sincerely,

[Name]
[Title]

When you get a name through a referral by someone else, always mention the referral right up front in your letter. This makes the reader pay a little more attention out of courtesy for their friend who clearly thought they might appreciate this information for a reason.

Prospect Referral 2

[Date]

[Name]
[Company]
[Address]
[City, State, Zip]

Dear:

I am the new area representative for [Company], and when visiting with [Name] at [Company] last week, he/she mentioned that I should contact you and introduce our products.

We have been providing cleaning services to all the major office and industrial parks in the county, and I'd like to find out if we can be of assistance to your company as well.

Our staff are bonded, professional, courteous, and, most importantly, attentive to detail. Whether your needs are occasional cleaning, regular cleaning services, or a special project such as seasonal "top to bottom" cleaning and touch-ups, we have the program to meet your needs.

[Name] mentioned that you prefer that appointments of this nature be scheduled through your secretary, so I will give her a call next week to set up a meeting at your convenience.

I am looking forward to meeting you, and hope that you will be open to considering our service.

Sincerely,

[Name]
[Title]

This letter even goes further than just naming the person who referred them, but also mentions specific ways the prospect likes to do business.

Prospect Using Competitor 1

[Date]

[Name]
[Company]
[Address]
[City, State, Zip]

Dear:

Today's call center technology is becoming increasingly sophisticated, but there is one critical item that has stayed relatively the same: a headset that offers quality sound, every call.

Our new product, [Name], has the key functions every agent needs: comfortable fit, a quick disconnect that will come apart when you need it, and stay together when you need that, and a noise-canceling microphone.

We'd like you to consider trying our products, so that you know what the competition offers, and have an alternate resource when you need it.

We're not going to waste your time, or ours, talking about the other fine products that are available today; rather, we prefer to let our product speak for itself.

For a free trial offer, simply fill out the enclosed card, and one of our agents will contact you. Once we determine which of our models and amplifiers will work best for you, we'll send you a complete agent headset kit for a 30-day evaluation.

We're sure you will find our product comparable to what you are currently using. We look forward to your putting our headsets to the test!

Sincerely,

[Name]
[Title]

> Be sure to remind readers of the need for what you are selling and put the benefits of your product right up front.

Prospect Using Competitor 2

[Date]

[Name]
[Company]
[Address]
[City, State, Zip]

Dear:

[Company] is one of the oldest and most respected forms distributors in the industry. We have quality stock forms at competitive pricing, and the ability to produce custom preprinted forms to your specifications.

Unlike other forms distributors, we do not require you to sign a multi-year contract, and, even more important, we have kept our price increases to a minimum and our service at maximum.

If you are tired of being locked into a paper contract where the pricing increases as soon as you sign, if you want your representative to contact you, every time you need them, give [Company] a try. Since we won't make you sign a contract, you truly have nothing to lose, and much to gain.

Call us, today.

Sincerely,

[Name]
[Title]

You don't have to name names and you don't have to get too negative, but just a little reminder that your competitor's products or services are a little less convenient than yours can be a key deciding factor.

Former Customer Letter 1

[Date]

[Name]
[Company]
[Address]
[City, State, Zip]

Dear:

It's been some time since we have heard from you, and even longer since your last order. We value you as our customer, and we'd like to regain your trust and your business.

As the new Sales Manager for [Company], I want to understand the relationship between our company and customers. I would like to meet with you to learn what we did right over the years, where we could have done better, and what we can do to reestablish our relationship.

I'll be visiting the area next month, and would like to set up an appointment with you. I'll call you next week to set up a meeting, and take the first step in renewing our ties with you.

Sincerely,

[Name]
[Title]

Former customers are some of the most valuable prospects you can have.

Former Customer Letter 2

[Date]

[Name]
[Company]
[Address]
[City, State, Zip]

Dear:

[Company] is back in business! We have completed the rebuilding of our manufacturing and distribution operations after the fire last year, and we are ready to start running 2 full shifts. We have been touched by the kindness shown to us by our competitors, in stepping in to keep our customers' stock needs satisfied. We know that you have been served well by these fine businesses, and some of you may feel that it is better to maintain your relationship with them.

That being said, we would like the opportunity to regain your business! Our Sales Manager will be contacting each of our customers in the coming months, and we look forward to resuming our relationship with each of you.

Thank you, as well, for the trust you have placed in us over the years through your business. It is not something we have ever taken for granted, but have truly appreciated.

Sincerely,

[Name]
[Title]

Rebuilding a business can mean a significant loss in your customer base. But when you are up and running again, be sure to make big noise about it to everyone who has ever bought anything from you!

Chapter 7

Letters Requesting a Sales Appointment

A letter can be the common courtesy that sets you apart from your competitors. Potential customers appreciate a letter giving them some options for appointment times, and a heads up that you plan to call.

While you could do this kind of thing via e-mail, a letter also gives you the chance to send some handpicked sales literature that the potential customer might find useful to look over before they meet with you. Never miss out on an opportunity to hand out the literature that you worked hard to put together and spent lots of money printing. The literature should be out there working for you as much as possible.

Personal Contact

Your advance letter to set up an appointment should remind the customer if you have already spoken. It is always a good idea to put any personal contact reminders up front in the letter— either personal contact with you or with someone who referred them to you or you to them. This kind of information will help ensure they will keep reading.

The Benefit

Always get the benefit to the customer into your letter as early as possible. After reminding them of where you made contact, remind them what product or service they expressed interest in or that you thought they would be interested in based on what they said.

Then briefly outline the benefits that they will enjoy once they have purchased your product or service. Don't tell them everything—you have to save something for the in-person appointment—but explain enough to intrigue them and allow them to look forward to your visit.

The Literature

Tell the reader what literature you are enclosing with the letter. Explain why you are enclosing it. And tell them what in it they should specifically look at. For example, "You mentioned you were interested in something different for fixtures. If you look at page 4, you will see our unique line of showerheads and sink fixtures that could help give your bathroom the unique touches you are looking for."

Suggest Times

Let your customer know if there are specific times that you are in their area. If it is easy enough for you to get to them at any time, then suggest a couple of possibilities, but otherwise let them pick a time for a meeting.

Their Place or Yours

Typically you would probably want to go to the customer—it is always better to make it as convenient for them as you can. But if they can get to you without much hassle and you have a showroom or otherwise can offer a better selection of samples to view, by all means try to have the meeting take place at your showroom. If you have a web site, certainly mention it but don't make your customer do all the legwork. And if there are things that need explanation, they might get turned off thinking you don't have what they want, without you there to explain things to them.

Specials

In this letter, let your customer know about any incentives or discounts they might miss out on if they don't schedule the appointment before the special is over. This is a great way to get them to set up an appointment soon.

Helping Them

Your letter should not just exude your desire to sell the customer something. Your should also indicate that you are trying to help your customer solve a problem. This can be done better after you have had a chance to ask some pointed questions to lead you to what problem they may have that you could solve. You are always looking to be your customer's solution to a problem.

Letter Style

The tone of the letter requesting an appointment should be friendly, approachable, and light. You want them to want to see you, not dread having to sit with a boring salesperson who is only looking to make money selling them something. Even though your letter sounds friendly, make sure it is also professional and accurate, both in information and in spelling and grammar.

Appointment Following Cold Call 1

This is a very succinct letter that includes all the key elements to entice a potential customer to agree to an appointment. It is friendly but professional, includes a reminder of their previous contact, and gives a specific day when the salesperson plans to call to set up an appointment.

[Date]

[Name]
[Company]
[Address]
[City, State, Zip]

Dear:

Thanks for taking my call today. I feel confident after discussing your current needs that our products would exceed your expectations.

I would like to arrange for an appointment so that I can show you samples of our product line, and can review our warehousing and stock order programs.

I will call you on Friday to set up a meeting. I look forward to continuing our discussions.

Sincerely,

[Name]
[Title]

Appointment Following Cold Call 2

[Date]

[Name]
[Company]
[Address]
[City, State, Zip]

Dear:

I'm glad I had the opportunity to meet you yesterday, when I was visiting the purchasing manager at [Company]. It was clear that I caught you at a bad time, and I appreciate the courtesy you showed in spite of all that was going on.

May I call on you next week in a more convenient time for you, so that I can show you our fall collection? I will call your office [Day and Date] so that we can set a time and a brief agenda for our meeting.

Thanks again for speaking with me. I appreciate it.

Sincerely,

[Name]
[Title]

It is often better to acknowledge something like catching someone "at a bad time" than to ignore it. People appreciate acknowledgment that you understand their busy schedule.

Appointment Following Letter of Introduction 1

[Date]

[Name]
[Company]
[Address]
[City, State, Zip]

Dear:

[Name] was kind enough to present a letter of introduction for me when she was at your office last week. I would like to schedule an appointment with you at your earliest convenience. I am looking for an internship opportunity for the summer of my Junior Year, and your company was suggested to me as one that provides a wide range of marketing and design project work.

I am including my transcripts and GPA for your review, and will call you Tuesday to set up a meeting. I am excited about the chance to gain experience working for [Company]

Sincerely,

[Name]
[Title]

This potential intern has included his or her transcripts that allow the recipient to look this information over before they talk on the phone.

Appointment Following Letter of Introduction 2

[Date]

[Name]
[Company]
[Address]
[City, State, Zip]

Dear:

I am writing to you as a follow-up to the letter of introduction presented to you by [Name] when they visited with you last month.

I am one of several partners who have developed and plan to market a new software product designed to automate receivable and payable functions for the SOHO (small office home office) marketplace.

I would like to make an appointment with you, at your earliest convenience, to discuss our business plan, and, more importantly to secure your commitment to act as our spokesperson in the media.

You are a respected member of the business community whose opinion is highly regarded. My partners and I feel that having you represent our product will provide the credibility we desire in the SOHO Marketplace.

I look forward to speaking with and meeting you in the near future.

Sincerely,

[Name]
[Title]

This letter acknowledges the recipient's place in the community as a business leader without being too overly gushy. It gives just enough information about the product to entice the potential spokesperson to want to hear more.

Appointment to Make a Specific Presentation 1

[Date]

[Name]
[Company]
[Address]
[City, State, Zip]

Dear:

In the past few months my partners and I have worked hard to develop a business, sales, and marketing plan. We have secured our first-level financing, and are planning to move ahead with our product announcements in the next six weeks.

My partners and I would like to meet with you to present our business plan in its entirety. We are offering this "sneak peek" to a select few associates who have been generous with their time and experience as we refined our product launch.

We are hosting a lunch and presentation on [Date] at [Location]. Please let us know if you plan to attend by returning the enclosed postcard. We appreciate that you have kept our confidence thus far, and look forward to being able to share the entire plan with you.

Sincerely,

[Name]
[Title]

Everyone loves a free lunch. Be sure to make it easy for them to reply by enclosing a self-addressed stamped reply card on which they only need to check yes or no.

Appointment to Make a Specific Presentation 2

[Date]

[Name]
[Company]
[Address]
[City, State, Zip]

Dear:

The Board of Directors of [Organization], together with the President and Senior Staff, cordially invite you to join us on [Date], for our annual shareholders meeting.

The purpose of the meeting is to review the year and how we met the goals and objectives outlined for us at last year's meeting. We have high expectations for the coming year, and an important part of this meeting will be to present the new product line, as well as our planned marketing campaigns.

A complete agenda for this meeting is enclosed. We hope that you can attend this meeting in person. If other commitments will keep you from attending in person, we are making this meeting accessible by streaming video on our web site.

Please confirm your attendance by [Date].

Sincerely,

[Name]
[Title]

Shareholders' meetings are mandatory for public companies. Provide an agenda as a courtesy and expect RSVPs.

Appointment Introducing a New Sales Promotion 1

[Date]

[Name]
[Company]
[Address]
[City, State, Zip]

Dear:

I'm pleased to announce that [Company] has created an exciting new promotional opportunity for our customers, for the 4th quarter.

In response to the positive response to our 3rd quarter cash promotion for the sale of [Product], we are extending this promotion to the 4th quarter, and we have added a number of incentives that will give your salespeople the opportunity to double, and triple their incentive rewards.

I'd like to schedule a meeting with your sales team, to go over the specifics of this promotion, and to kick off our new incentive program with a $100.00 cash drawing. I know that you generally have sales and training meetings on Friday mornings, so if it's appropriate for me to meet with your team on one of those days, just let me know.

I'm very excited that this program is continuing into what is historically the busiest quarter of the year. Please let me know when is a convenient time for me to visit.

Sincerely,

[Name]
[Title]

Keeping salespeople apprised of any specials and incentives for sales is crucial. Try fitting into one of their usual sales meetings. And offering a cash drawing is always a good gesture!

Appointment Introducing a New Sales Promotion 2

[Date]

[Name]
[Company
[Address]
[City, State, Zip]

Dear:

[Name] Laundry and Dry Cleaning is now open for business! We are located at [Address] and offer full-size laundromat, dry cleaning, mending and alteration services, and seasonal storage.

As an introductory offer, we are offering a "clean one, clean two" dry cleaning promotion. For every item of clothing brought to us for dry cleaning, we will clean a like item at no charge. For example, bring 2 blazers, pay for one cleaning, and so on.

This promotion is open to all personnel in our office building, for the month of [Month], for unlimited visits. I would like to set up an appointment to come in and introduce our services and this special to your staff sometime next week. I will call you on Friday to see if we can arrange a convenient time.

We'll be offering additional services in the coming months, such as pick-up and delivery from local offices, and more.

We look forward to your patronage.

Sincerely,

[Name]
[Title]

Explain your business and any significant promotion in person whenever possible.

Appointment to Introduce a New Salesperson 1

A longtime salesperson becomes a key asset to a company. When that person leaves it is very helpful for a smooth transition and lack of interruption in sales if they can personally introduce their replacement to their accounts.

[Date]

[Name]
[Company]
[Address]
[City, State, Zip]

Dear:

Thank you for your note and your kind words regarding my pending retirement. While I am looking forward to spending more time with my family, and traveling for pleasure rather than business, my retirement is bittersweet, knowing that the day-to-day interaction with my customers and my friends, such as you, will come to an end.

I am pleased to report that [Company] has hired my successor, and I would like to make an appointment to introduce [him/her] personally. [Name] has worked in our industry for [number] years, most recently with [Company]. I'm sure you'll find [him/her] well versed in our products and eager to meet your requirements.

Please let me know if we can meet with you next week, and if there is a particular day or time that works best for you. As always, I look forward to seeing you, and to "passing the torch" on to [Name]. I am confident you will be in good hands.

Sincerely,

[Name]
[Title]

Appointment to Introduce a New Salesperson 2

[Date]

[Name]
[Company]
[Address]
[City, State, Zip]

Dear:

Thank you for your reorder! I appreciate the trust you place in me, as your representative, and our company as a whole through your continued business.

In addition to my regular duties as area sales representative, I am also responsible for training some of our sales interns. I will be traveling with [Name], who is in training to provide sales and support to the western part of our state.

I'd like to stop by and see you in 2 weeks, so that I can go over the inventory and let you know where you may want to focus your next reorder. With your permission, I'd like to bring [Name] along, introduce [him/her], and give [him/her] some hands-on experience in dealing with premium clients.

I'll call you the day before we plan to be in town, to make sure our plans are convenient. Please call me if you have any questions.

Sincerely,

[Name]
[Title]

Always let an appointment know that you are bringing someone along with you. It is a common courtesy.

Appointment to Introduce a New Product

Introducing a new product before the sales reps start making calls to sell it can generate solid interest in the product.

[Date]

[Name]
[Company]
[Address]
[City, State, Zip]

Dear:

For months our customers have been asking for this, and we are pleased to announce that we have built a better mousetrap!

The new Have-A Heart Mousetrap takes the place of the older more traditional animal traps. Animal and environmentally safe, this easy-to-use trap will help capture the unwanted visitors in your home or office, for safe and clean removal.

We will be taking orders for limited shipping beginning next month. Our sales representatives will be calling on our customers next week to set up appointments and demonstrations.

We hope you will find time to meet with your sales rep, and place your order! Have-A-Heart is a trademark of the "Kill Them" brand of animal control tools.

Sincerely,

[Name]
[Title]

Appointment to Introduce a New Service

[Date]

[Name]
[Company]
[Address]
[City, State, Zip]

Dear:

[Name] auto dealership is proud to announce a new service. Our team of professional, factory-trained service men and women will now detail your car, as part of your annual maintenance and state inspection.

Our staff will inspect your car and work with you to assure that it will pass inspection. While we are maintaining your vehicle, our staff will also clean the interior, wash and wax the exterior, and detail your vehicle, all in the same day.

To take advantage of this special introductory offer, make your appointment now, to have your car inspected and refurbished.

We look forward to seeing you, and your vehicle!

Sincerely,

[Name]
[Title]

A promotional tool like this is definitely worth a letter in advance!

Brief Outline of Sales Presentation 1

[Date]

[Name]
[Company]
[Address]
[City, State, Zip]

Dear:

Thank you for taking my call today. I am looking forward to meeting with you on Tuesday, and this letter is to confirm the agenda for our meeting.

I would like to take about 45 minutes of your time, and review the following:

- Overview of Company History
- Product Information
- Features and Benefits of the Product
- Competitive Analysis
- Pricing Structures and Leasing Options

Of course, any questions you might have will be addressed at our meeting as well. I appreciate your willingness to meet with me, and will see you on [Day and Date].

Sincerely,

[Name]
[Title]

> A letter outlining an agenda for a meeting is a professional way to ensure that you are not going to be wasting someone's time.

Brief Outline of Sales Presentation 2

[Date]

[Name]
[Company]
[Address]
[City, State, Zip]

Dear:

Thank you for your interest in our distribution and channel partner opportunities. Enclosed is basic information that you should know about how our relationships work in the reseller channel.

During our meeting on Monday, I will have a more detailed outline of what we expect from partners, and, in turn, what we offer for support. We can talk about pricing, minimums, and shipping and handling fees, as well as the region you will be supporting.

I will have my Sales Manager, [Name], with me, so that we can finalize our agreement once our presentation is complete.

I'm looking forward to seeing you on Monday.

Sincerely,

[Name]
[Title]

A preview of an impending meeting helps the other party prepare any questions they might have, including soliciting comments and questions from other people in the company that won't be in the meeting.

Chapter 8

Cover Letters

Cover letters are important not always for what they say in the copy of the letter itself but in the fact that they show a professionalism that people expect. To open an envelope and have a brochure, catalog, or proposal drop out without any introductory letter seems sloppy on the part of the salesperson. And sloppiness of any kind often says to a prospective customer that you may perhaps be a little sloppy in the work you do.

Keep It Simple

A cover letter does not have to repeat everything that is in the enclosed materials. In fact, it shouldn't—why would the reader bother opening the literature if the cover letter seems to tell it all? But what it should do is remind the recipient why they are receiving the materials—they requested it at a trade show, in a phone call, from your web site. And you should point out any specific items or features that are in the literature that the customer might be especially interested in. This should be no more than a two- or three-sentence paragraph. End your letter with an offer to visit their establishment with samples or for them to come visit your showroom. If neither of those is possible, direct them to your company's web site and offer to call and arrange a phone appointment in which you can go over their needs in detail.

Tone

The tone of your sales cover letters should be professional but personable. Be accurate in both your statements and your punctuation and grammar. Don't be so breezy casual that you use words like "ain't." But also don't be so formal as to be intimidating (unless of course you are selling leather-bound classic literature to Ivy League professors or something that should sound a little formal!). Basically, be yourself. Let the reader get a taste of what it might be like to meet with you in person—which is often exactly what you are going to ask them to do.

In Closing

The sales cover letter is not the place to close the sale. This you want to do in person, whether in person means actually standing side-by-side or talking over the phone. Your cover letter should lead to a closing, however, if your interactions thus far have led to this point. If you are sending follow-up materials having narrowed down what the customer is interested in, then the last sentence in your cover letter should be something like "Can I call you Friday afternoon to get your order?"

Cover Letter for Sales Promotion Material 1

[Date]

[Name]
[Company]
[Address]
[City, State, Zip]

Dear:

Thank you for signing up for our promotional event taking place in December. We are committed to making this a winning opportunity for you, and want to do whatever we can to help train and motivate your staff.

Included with this letter is a full sales kit with posters, pricing, sample press releases, and product information to help your sales group sell space at the upcoming trade show.

Our team of specialists are available by phone to answer any questions you have, and once you select the posters and other advertisements you want to use, our marketing staff will print them out, complete with your logo and company contact information.

Don't hesitate to call once you have reviewed the material. I will follow up next week to make sure you are ready to start.

Sincerely,

[Name]
[Title]

This cover letter lists what promotional material the receiver should expect to find enclosed. It also assures the recipient that support personnel are as close as a phone call.

Cover Letter for Sales Promotion Material 2

[Date]

[Name]
[Company]
[Address]
[City, State, Zip]

Dear:

The information you requested concerning our equipment rebate program is enclosed! We're excited to be able to offer this opportunity to receive a rebate for upgrading your printers to our new multi-function units.

Once you have had a chance to look at the options for printers, call our technical service department and they will schedule an appointment to evaluate and service your existing units, so that we can determine fair market trade for an upgraded model.

Don't hesitate to call if you have any questions.

Sincerely,

[Name]
[Title]

Never send out any literature without a cover letter. As this letter shows, it can be a very simple letter that explains what is enclosed and encourages the recipient to call and schedule an appointment.

Cover Letter for Catalog 1

This letter provides a follow-up to materials requested as a result of visiting a web site. Be prepared with printed literature to back up your online presence.

[Date]

[Name]
[Company]
[Address]
[City, State, Zip]

Dear:

Thank you for visiting our web site and requesting a catalog. Enclosed you will find our full line kit, which covers all our stock products, as well as provides an overview of our custom ordering capabilities.

I will follow up with you next week to go over the material and answer any questions you might have. Thank you for your interest in [Company]. I look forward to speaking with you.

Sincerely,

[Name]
[Title]

Cover Letter for Catalog 2

[Date]

[Name]
[Company]
[Address]
[City, State, Zip]

Dear:

Thank you for your call. I have enclosed our catalog, and tabbed several pages that have the type of components you indicated were of interest. These are available for immediate delivery.

Since you have not done business with us before, I have taken the liberty of including a credit application, so that you can take advantage of our 2% 5, Net 30 terms. I will call you next week but please don't hesitate to contact me right away if you have questions.

Sincerely,

[Name]
[Title]

Pointing out that you have highlighted items in a catalog that would be of interest to potential customers is a great way to let them see that you are willing to make things easy for them.

Cover Letter for Seasonal Catalog 1

Point out any significant items in catalogs that you send, like those items that are going to be phased out.

[Date]

[Name]
[Company]
[Address]
[City, State, Zip]

Dear:

Happy Holidays! We are pleased to send you our annual Holiday Catalog, especially designed for companies that want to remember a large customer base on a small budget. Last year's very popular candy jar is back again, and we can imprint this clear glass jar with your logo in black, silver, or gold.

Take a look at the new items as well as a few old favorites that will be phased out after this holiday season. The holiday rush is almost upon us! Don't delay!

Sincerely,

[Name]
[Title]

Cover Letter for Seasonal Catalog 2

[Date]

[Name]
[Company]
[Address]
[City, State, Zip]

Dear:

We know it's hard to think about working outside when the temperatures are in the single digits, but we also know that no matter how much we think winter will never end, spring is right around the corner!

It's almost time to think about your spring planting, annual flowers, vegetables, and decorative trees and shrubs.

Look over the enclosed catalog, watch the snowfall, and remember, spring is only a few months away!

Sincerely,

[Name]
[Title]

Use a cover letter to get recipients excited about looking inside your catalog.

Cover Letter for Brochure 1

[Date]

[Name]
[Company]
[Address]
[City, State, Zip]

Dear:

Thank you for your interest in our conference and seminar function rooms. The enclosed brochure has information on our 3 conference rooms, including electrical, audio, and video capabilities.

We'd like to invite you to tour our facility and see for yourself why companies are taking their meetings off-site, and letting us host their corporate or customer events. We look forward to hosting yours as well!

Sincerely,

[Name]
[Title]

This simple letter lets readers know what is enclosed and offers a quick invitation to come look for themselves.

Cover Letter for Brochure 2

[Date]

[Name]
[Company]
[Address]
[City, State, Zip]

Dear:

Our corporate limousine fleet is growing! We've added a new 24-foot Mercedes stretch limo with all the comforts for executive travel. Satellite TV, phone, and Internet access are just a few of the amenities that we have to offer.

As the enclosed brochure indicates, this is the perfect way to impress a client, reward a top achiever, or simply travel in style.

We hope you will consider our services for your corporate travel needs.

Sincerely,

[Name]
[Title]

Something like a top-class stretch limo is hard to do justice to with words. Always include a brochure and use a cover letter to entice readers to look inside.

Cover Letter for Flyer 1

[Date]

[Name]
[Company]
[Address]
[City, State, Zip]

Dear:

Our popular "Truckload Meat Sale" will take place the last weekend in September! We've purchased enough beef, pork, and chicken to feed an army. As you can see from the enclosed flyer, we have a variety of packages available, to fit every family and every budget.

From our "beef lovers" package to the "oversized family variety pack," we think there is something for everyone. Stop by during our sale, or, if you prefer, use the order form on the back page of the flyer and let us know what you want, and when you want it.

We'll have everything packed up for you, so you can go home and store it whatever way works best for you.

See you at the meat counter!

Sincerely,

[Name]
[Title]

Explain what you have enclosed and how they should use it. In this case, not only is there a list of what is being offered but there is an order form that can be filled out.

Cover Letter for Flyer 2

[Date]

[Name]
[Company]
[Address]
[City, State, Zip]

Dear:

The PTA will once again sponsor a "Santa's Shopping Day" for parents and children in our kindergarten and elementary schools. On [Date] children will have the chance to do some Christmas shopping from a wide range of crafts and small gifts made by local artisans. We'll even help them wrap their gifts so they can surprise Mom and Dad!

We hope you will show your support for the artists listed on our flyer, as they are donating their time and materials! Proceeds from this event will help fund additional PTA events.

Your PTA wishes you the best of the holiday season.

Sincerely,

[Name]
[Title]

A cover letter can serve to further explain a flyer and show the enthusiasm of those involved in a project like this one.

Cover Letter for Proposal 1

[Date]

[Name]
[Company]
[Address]
[City, State, Zip]

Dear:

Thank you for considering [Company] for your printing needs. I am enclosing a price proposal that outlines the scope of work I will perform, benchmark tests, and a final report. I think it covers what you indicated were your most critical needs for this first phase, but if I have missed anything please let me know.

I appreciate the opportunity to provide you with this quote, and I look forward to your feedback.

Sincerely,

[Name]
[Title]

A proposal and price quote should always include a brief cover letter.

Cover Letter for Proposal 2

[Date]

[Name]
[Company]
[Address]
[City, State, Zip]

Dear:

This is in response to your request for a bid for network equipment and software. We believe we have met the requirements your bid specifies and have answered all questions satisfactorily. We feel confident that we are able to exceed your expectations with the enclosed proposal, and look forward to your favorable response.

Sincerely,

[Name]
[Title]

Sometimes materials speak for themselves. This cover letter doesn't need to say much in the text, but what it says by its presence is that you are a professional who doesn't send stuff out without a personal letter introducing the enclosures.

Chapter 9

Sales Proposal Letters

Your sales job will most likely include proposing opportunities to potential customers. There are many ways to entice people with your proposals.

Coupons

Including a coupon with your sales pitch to a prospective customer is a great way not only to get response but to track responses as well. Customers love coupons—they feel like they are getting something for nothing. Make your coupons worthwhile. Don't expect people to cash in a coupon and try something out that saves them just a few cents.

Special Offers

Special promotions are another way to attract undecided customers and get them to at least try your product or service. Find something that isn't a huge cost to you but seems significant to potential customers—and is significant. For a customer to sign on to a bigger arrangement with you, for example to do all their company printing under a year-long contract, offer to let them try you out first on a smaller project for a significant discount. It can end up being a win-win situation for everyone.

Solicited Proposals

Sometimes your proposals will be solicited. A current or new customer will ask you to put together a contract or proposal for something they know they want. Don't consider these much easier of a sale to close than the unsolicited proposal you put together for the potential customer who didn't even know you existed before you contacted them. While you don't have to do as much convincing of the customer who solicited the proposal, you haven't closed the deal until all the names are signed and the deposit is made. And you don't necessarily know (although you should ask!) who else they are asking to do proposals for them.

Unsolicited Proposals

Most of the time you, the salesperson, will be going out and soliciting potential business, offering to put together contracts and proposals for work. These will require more upfront work and more follow-up and a more detailed letter along with the proposal. Many of the details should have been discussed in phone conversations and meetings prior to the proposal stage, but you should always reiterate any details that you think the client really ought to know, even if it is in the proposal. You never know in how much detail clients read proposals and contracts.

Letter Proposing a Special Offer 1

[Date]

[Name]
[Company]
[Address]
[City, State, Zip]

Dear:

[Name] magazine, a monthly publication reporting on business news for the state of [State], would like you to consider advertising with us.

Our demographic information is enclosed, but briefly, our publication reaches a monthly circulation of [amount] and our readers are professionals in a variety of vertical markets throughout the state.

Our advertisers report new prospects as a result of advertising in our magazine, as well as renewed contact with existing customers. Would you like to take advantage of this chance to increase your business through advertising?

For a limited time only, we are making this special offer to new advertisers. Place an ad in our magazine for 2 months, and we'll run the same ad for a 3rd month at no charge. We will guarantee placement on the same page for the 3rd month, so your customers will know where to find you!

Details can be found in the attached rate and circulation information. This is an offer that will sell out quickly, so don't delay; call us today, and increase your business using the power of advertising.

Sincerely,

[Name]
[Title]

Proposing a special introductory rate is a good way to bring in new customers.

Letter Proposing a Special Offer 2

[Date]

[Name]
[Company]
[Address]
[City, State, Zip]

Dear:

[Name] Office Supply store is proud to announce our grand opening in [City]. We are open for business, and want you to be our customer!

We have a special introductory offer for the back-to-school student, or anyone who is planning a printer purchase. Buy any HP printer, and we'll give you an extra set of ink cartridges at no charge. Ink cartridges that come with printers are typically "starter" units with only a small amount of ink. Replacement cartridges can cost more than $50.00, especially for the color units. We'll give you the standard ink cartridges for the model you purchase, at no extra cost.

We have a variety of specials in almost every department. Stop by, say hello to our staff, and stock up. We are also offering business accounts with free local delivery.

We are looking forward to seeing you in our new store!

Sincerely,

[Name]
[Title]

Introductory offers coinciding with a new store opening bring in new customers.

Letter Proposing a Contract 1

Being encouraged to submit a proposal is something not to be passed over, even if you are not sure you want the job! If it's a job you don't really want, you can propose hours, rates, or tasks that you know will be rejected. If you do want the job, be competitive and be enthusiastic with your cover letter.

[Date]

[Name]
[Company]
[Address]
[City, State, Zip]

Dear:

I have enjoyed working with your company on a freelance basis for the past month, and I feel we have made a good start toward creating a process and procedural manual that will be a part of your ISO Certification.

I've given some thought to your offer of continuing my association with [Company] and I have included a proposed contractual agreement for additional consulting services.

The contract outlines the scope of work that I would expect to accomplish during this extension of my tenure, and reviews the hours per week that I am able to commit to your organization.

I will give you a call early next week to discuss the terms and conditions, and look forward to your feedback.

Sincerely,

[Name]
[Title]

Letter Proposing a Contract 2

[Date]

[Name]
[Company]
[Address]
[City, State, Zip]

Dear:

Thank you for the time you took to review our proposal for contract manufacturing. I feel that our plant has the equipment and the capabilities that you require, and I would like to finalize our agreement.

Enclosed is the proposed contract that outlines the scope of work, as well as the confidentiality clauses you requested. I'm sure you would like your legal department to review it as well. If you find everything to your satisfaction, please initial, sign where indicated, and return both copies to me. I will sign and return one copy to you for your files.

If you have any questions concerning the language or intent of this contract, please do not hesitate to call.

Sincerely,

[Name]
[Title]

Preparing a contract and suggesting a legal review show that you know what you are doing and that you have done this before.

Letter Proposing a Trial Offer 1

[Date]

[Name]
[Company]
[Address]
[City, State, Zip]

Dear:

Thank you for visiting our web site and inquiring about our call center software. We feel that we offer state-of-the-art call capture technology, and would like you to see for yourself how our product can help track and identify inbound and outbound trends.

We'd like to offer you a chance to use our software on a trial basis. We currently have a program that allows participating prospects to download a full version of our software. You will be able to use all the features and functionality of this program for 14 days. At the end of the trial period, you can opt to purchase the product, and we will bill you [amount] and give you a permanent license.

To learn more, or to take advantage of this trial offer, log on to our web site, and fill out the acceptance form located at this link: [www.www.com/trial]. One of our technical support representatives will contact you to help you with the installation and answer any questions you have.

We look forward to hearing from you.

Sincerely,

[Name]
[Title]

Trial offers are great ways to bring in new customers. What better way to find out if a product is something you need than by trying it in real-world situations?

Letter Proposing a Trial Offer 2

[Date]

[Name]
[Company]
[Address]
[City, State, Zip]

Dear:

I'm convinced that the telemarketing software that is on the market today is not what most companies are looking for. The scripts are pre-written and the ability to have a free-flow conversation with a prospect is hampered by the requirements of "sticking to the script."

I have been providing telemarketing and lead generation services to local companies since [year], and I would like to show you how having an outsource lead generator will increase your number of qualified leads and generate more business.

I'm confident enough in my services that I am willing to work for four hours, at no charge, cold-calling from any list you have that you want prospected. I think the results that I can bring will outweigh any doubts you may have.

Please call me at the number on my card, and let me show you how you can generate new opportunities through a personal lead generator.

Sincerely,

[Name]
[Title]

Prove your success rate by giving a couple free hours of work.

Letter Proposing a Sale 1

To close a sale, provide everything the customer needs to get to the next stage of ordering the product or service. The more time they have to think about it, the more time they have to procrastinate and decide no or find reasons to use a competitor.

[Date]

[Name]
[Company]
[Address]
[City, State, Zip]

Dear:

I enjoyed speaking with you today, and the price quote you requested is enclosed. If you are ready to order these components you can purchase by credit card, or on our 2% 5, net 45 terms. A credit card form and a credit application are attached.

I look forward to receiving your order.

Sincerely,

[Name]
[Title]

Letter Proposing a Sale 2

[Date]

[Name]
[Company]
[Address]
[City, State, Zip]

Dear:

The evaluation period for the folding machine is almost at an end. I hope that since our technician adjusted the fold plates you have found it to run more efficiently at its rated speed. I am including an invoice and would ask that you sign off and return if you would like to purchase this unit.

The purchase of this unit entitles you to 90 days on-site service. Information on an extended warranty plan is also included for your convenience.

I hope you elect to keep this folder, but if for some reason you wish to return it, please notify me within 5 business days so that we can crate the unit and return it to the manufacturer.

Sincerely,

[Name]
[Title]

Following through with your offer to take items back that customers are dissatisfied with is a cost of doing business and proves you are worth doing business with.

Letter Proposing a Special Offer 1

[Date]

[Name]
[Company]
[Address]
[City, State, Zip]

Dear:

Thank you for taking the time to participate in our conference call today. We are excited about the possibilities of our joint partnership, and we have much to discuss in the days ahead.

One of the action items that came from our call today was a way to develop a more "interactive web site" for your customers to familiarize themselves with our products.

We understand that while you want customers to become more knowledgeable about the products we offer, you want them to think they are dealing with you, rather than visiting our web site. We have a program that we would like to put in place for you, which will accomplish both tasks.

We propose placing pages on your site with information on those products you will purchase from us. The "contact for more information" button will generate an e-mail to both of us, so that we can send the samples, in your name, and you can follow up with the customer.

This is a short-term solution while we address the dual web site you have requested. Let me now what you think.

Sincerely,

[Name]
[Title]

Use a letter to review what you discussed with the customer and the solutions you have come up with.

Letter Proposing a Special Offer 2

[Date]

[Name]
[Company]
[Address]
[City, State, Zip]

Dear:

Thank you for contacting me regarding your interest in our [product]. I am enclosing the pricing you asked for, and would like to confirm our discussion about a contingency purchase order.

Purchase orders of this nature are "real" and are provided to us as a confirmation that you have a valid interest in the product. The terms of a contingency purchase order are that "as long as the machine performs to its stated expectations, the client will then purchase the equipment, for the price listed on the purchase order."

Contingency purchase orders typically are for a 5-day business period. We will pay the freight charges to you, and should you keep the machine, the freight charges are "on us." If you decide to return the machine at the end of the evaluation period, you are responsible for freight both ways.

A contingency purchase order contract is attached for your convenience. Please let me know if you have any questions.

Sincerely,

[Name]
[Title]

Being very clear in writing about your purchasing policies can avoid miscommunication leading to a negative relationship later.

Letter Proposing a Special Offer 3

[Date]

[Name]
[Company]
[Address]
[City, State, Zip]

Dear:

We are pleased to announce that a special offer is in effect for customers who order their fall and winter footwear in July.

For those customers who order in the "fall program" and within the minimum guidelines, we will delay billing until October 1. After October 1, standard billing rates will apply.

We hope this change of terms helps you in your planning.

Sincerely,

[Name]
[Title]

Announce a change in terms to customers in writing, whether the changes are in their favor or not.

Letter Proposing a Trial Offer

[Date]

[Name]
[Company]
[Address]
[City, State, Zip]

Dear:

We are pleased to announce we are continuing our "buy one, get one free" program for toner. If you are currently purchasing toner from us, you have the opportunity receive a second toner cartridge for every one you buy, up to five toners.

Details are on the enclosed order form.

Sincerely,

[Name]
[Title]

Always make it clear in a letter if your special has a limit such as this one.

Letter Accompanying a Proposal 1

Keep track of bids you have out there, include a cover letter, and follow up on them in an appropriate time period.

[Date]

[Name]
[Company]
[Address]
[City, State, Zip]

Dear:

Thank you for the opportunity to participate in your bid process. We have completed all bid questions to the best of our ability, and the complete bid package is attached.

We appreciate your consideration, and look forward to your favorable response.

Sincerely,

[Name]
[Title]

Letter Accompanying a Proposal 2

[Date]

[Name]
[Company]
[Address]
[City, State, Zip]

Dear:

Our response to your request for information for software, hardware, and technical support has been submitted. We would like to thank the committee for the opportunity to showcase our products and services for your consideration. We look forward to your feedback.

Sincerely,

[Name]
[Title]

Send a written confirmation to the party you dealt with confirming that you sent the information you needed to send, especially if the information was to go to a third party.

Letter Proposing a Contract 1

[Date]

[Name]
[Company]
[Address]
[City, State, Zip]

Dear:

Thank you for your interest in my services as your consultant for the development of your telemarketing center. I have attached a boilerplate contract for you to review. It outlines the scope of services I will perform, what you can expect at the end of the contract period, and how we can measure my success at meeting your objectives.

Please let me know if you have any questions.

Sincerely,

[Name]
[Title]

Sending a sample boilerplate contract allows each party to start to tailor the contract to meet the needs of the specific job.

Letter Proposing a Contract 2

[Date]

[Name]
[Company]
[Address]
[City, State, Zip]

Dear:

I have enjoyed speaking with you and developing an outline for what you want in a Technical Support and Sales Manager, and I am including an invoice for my services to date.

I have also taken the liberty of including a contract for recruitment and salary negotiation of these two applicants. Please let me know if you are interested in using an outside source for placement, and what your thoughts are on the contract outline.

Although there are some things in the contract that we cannot negotiate, there are many things that are negotiable, so please do call with any questions.

Sincerely,

[Name]
[Title]

Proposals for work often need to include drawing up a sample contract. You should make it clear how negotiable the sample contract is.

Letter Proposing a Contract 3

[Date]

[Name]
[Company]
[Address]
[City, State, Zip]

Dear:

Attached please find for your review a contract outlining the terms and conditions for my service as an on-site consultant.

The scope of service that I will provide under the terms of this contract will be to develop a procedures manual for your inside sales and sales development personnel.

These manuals will be completed within a three-month period from the beginning date of service.

Thank you for allowing me to quote my services to your organization. Please let me know if you would like me to proceed.

Sincerely,

[Name]
[Title]

A contract will outline all the minor details but it is helpful for a cover letter to briefly mention a few of the key points up-front so the recipient will know that you are both on the same track about the main points.

Letter Proposing a Sale 1

[Date]

[Name]
[Company]
[Address]
[City, State, Zip]

Dear:

I have worked with my attorney to finalize a sales agreement for our manufacturing facility, buildings, and equipment, and the terms of the proposed sale are attached for your consideration.

I would like to finalize this sale by the end of the month, or move on to the next interested buyer. Please let me know if you are ready to commit to a purchase.

Sincerely,

[Name]
[Title]

You will have probably had this discussion already over the phone with the prospective buyer but it doesn't hurt to remind the purchaser of your timing considerations.

Letter Proposing a Sale 2

You would want to send this kind of letter and agreement via some overnight service with tracking service and at least delivery confirmation so you can be assured of the recipient getting it. Also, put a note in your calendar to call a couple days before the proposed meeting if you haven't heard from the other party.

[Date]

[Name]
[Company]
[Address]
[City, State, Zip]

Dear:

Thank you for your call today, and for taking the time to discuss options for the land sale in the [City] industrial park. I have attached a sales agreement that I think covers all the details we talked about. I would like to meet with you and our bankers on [Day] to formalize this agreement. Please let me know if you can make this meeting.

Sincerely,

[Name]
[Title]

Letter Proposing a Special Offer 1

[Date]

[Name]
[Company]
[Address]
[City, State, Zip]

Dear:

We are [Company], an independent lead generator and qualifier serving the software industry since [year]. We have a large and diverse talent pool that are trained in a variety of platforms, and have the ability to understand the needs of a prospect and translate that to an opportunity.

Are you seeking ways to increase the number of qualified leads your salespeople close? Give us a try! See the attached brochure for details on our great track record. You're one phone call away from more qualified sales leads.

Sincerely,

[Name]
[Title]

When selling something like a lead qualifying service, always mention you have an excellent track record whose specifics can be found in your enclosed brochure. Salespeople on all sides of the table like numbers.

Letter Proposing a Special Offer 2

When you are soliciting business for something like catering, suggest customers try you on a smaller scale before deciding about their important event. Coupons and free samples are always a good draw for getting new customers to try your service.

[Date]

[Name]
[Company]
[Address]
[City, State, Zip]

Dear:

It's time for companies to start planning their holiday parties, and sometimes it's difficult to locate a caterer that can provide quality food at an affordable price.

"Lettuce Entertain You" is the only completely vegetarian catering service in the valley. Enclosed is a complete list of the items we offer, along with sample menus and prices. Give us a try with the attached coupon, good for an appetizer platter valued at $50.00, for your next meeting. We think you'll find our fresh, organic vegetarian appetizers and entrees just what you've been looking for.

Sincerely,

[Name]
[Title]

Letter Proposing a Special Offer 3

[Date]

[Name]
[Company]
[Address]
[City, State, Zip]

Dear:

Have you ever tried to make a sales call and struggled for just the right thing to say? We think our book *Sales Scripts for the Tongue-Tied* has a variety of sales scripts for every industry, and every occasion.

If you are interested in trying our book, with no obligation, visit the following link: www.ww.com, and download up to 10 scripts at no charge.

We think, once you've tried them, you'll never be tongue-tied again!

Sincerely,

[Name]
[Title]

The Internet has become a great tool for letting people try out pieces of printed material, whether it's sales scripts or photographs.

Chapter 10

Follow-up Letters

Never underestimate the importance of the follow-up letter. This is where you get a chance to prove to a potential client that you are reliable, remember details, and heard what they said to you.

Literature

If the client asked you to send literature, send literature. Send what they requested as well as anything else you think would support the information they want. Send a cover letter explaining the literature at least briefly. Point out any specifics that you particularly want to bring to their attention, such as whether new colors of a product are available since the brochure was printed or if a product shown is no longer available.

Specifics

Let the customer know in the letter exactly what needs to happen next. If you are following up with a proposal, draft contract, or other documentation you promised, state in the letter how long the proposal is good for. Include a time when you will be back in touch to find out their response to the proposal and if they have further questions before you close the deal.

Counter Objections

The follow-up letter is a great opportunity to counter objections. If things came up in your personal meeting that a potential customer questioned as an issue for them, a letter can further clarify why this is a non-issue and what your company does about the problem. And you can certainly outline a few ideas for making the product or service more in line with their budget, if cost is an issue (and when isn't it?).

Courtesy Letters

If there is no specific further action needed, still follow up with a thank-you letter for taking up someone's time either on the phone or in person, for getting a tour of their facility, or for whatever courtesy they have shown you.

Short and Sweet

Keep your follow-up letters short. If you have something specific to relate, relate it and wrap it up. Say only what you need to say, include some general courtesies, and let the fact that you sent the letter at all speak for itself.

> Always include a business card with every letter you send. You don't need to mention it in the letter at all, but by including it you give the customer the opportunity to keep your contact information handy.

After the Sale

Don't forget your customer after the sale takes place or they accept your proposal or sign an agreement. The best customers you have are your current customers. Keep them happy and keep them thinking about you when they need what you offer. Send follow-up letters after they have made purchases—and encourage add-on purchases. Did they buy light fixtures from you? If you sell light bulbs, remind them they will need some. Did you sell them printed materials? Remind them that they should keep tabs on their inventory in order to not run out at a critical time. Or that the printed materials could be easily updated. Customers like knowing that their suppliers care about their business.

Letter to Follow Up an Appointment 1

Follow-up letters should be short, but be sure to be specific about what you discussed, what happens next, and when you plan to next be in touch.

[Date]

[Name]
[Company]
[Address]
[City, State, Zip]

Dear:

I appreciate the courtesy you extended during our meeting on Tuesday. I wanted to outline the action items we agreed upon so that we can continue our discussions accordingly.

I will look into the statistics you requested, as far as MTBF (mean time between failures) and the life cycle of the motherboards.

You will speak with your internal technical group and determine what the most common failure has been on your existing equipment, and provide me with the maintenance schedule your engineers have followed.

I should have my information for you by the end of the week, and will send it via e-mail. I will plan to call you next Thursday so that we can schedule our follow-up appointment.

Sincerely,

[Name]
[Title]

Letter to Follow Up an Appointment 2

[Date]

[Name]
[Company]
[Address]
[City, State, Zip]

Dear:

Thank you for your time last week. I appreciate the tour of the plant and have a better understanding of your marketing plans and what your needs are.

I have included some information on industry statistics for acceptable return rates on the mailings we discussed. I am putting a presentation together for your marketing team and would like to schedule a convenient time to present to your group.

I will be back in your area [day range] of next week. Please let me know if one of those days is appropriate for a follow-up meeting.

Sincerely,

[Name]
[Title]

Follow-up letters often include some materials that you promised you'd send. Always send what you said you would. Take notes during your meeting or phone call so you know for sure what those materials are.

Letter to Follow Up a Written Proposal 1

[Date]

[Name]
[Company]
[Address]
[City, State, Zip]

Dear:

I haven't been able to reach you by telephone, but I wanted to follow up regarding the stock product proposal I sent you last week.

As you can see from the pricing, it is a competitively priced product based on the volumes you anticipate. Freight costs would depend on the method of shipment; once you determine how you want it shipped I can provide you with an estimate.

I look forward to your favorable response, and to receiving your order.

Sincerely,

[Name]
[Title]

If a phone call fails, send a letter. First-class postal service is pretty quick, but if you want it to arrive immediately, the letter can be faxed or e-mailed or e-mailed as an attachment.

Letter to Follow Up a Written Proposal 2

[Date]

[Name]
[Company]
[Address]
[City, State, Zip]

Dear:

Have you had a chance to consider the proposal I sent you for the upgrade of your loading dock? I know that you were under a time constraint to get the work done before winter, and because of a scheduling conflict with another client, I have a three-week window available to perform the work to your specifications.

The pricing I proposed is good for 30 days from the date of the quote. Materials are in stock, and I have a crew ready to work.

Please let me know if you would like to proceed. I have another client interested in scheduling my crew, but I wanted to give you first option, since your request was ahead of the other client.

Sincerely,

[Name]
[Title]

If things change with a proposal, follow up with a letter outlining changes. You should probably call too and talk this over in person, but a letter is always a good way to have anything specific in written record.

Letter to Follow Up a Presentation 1

Presentations can be followed up with a letter that suggests other presentations you can do, continuing in the same vein. And it is always a courtesy to thank the host for the opportunity to present and to welcome any questions.

[Date]

[Name]
[Company]
[Address]
[City, State, Zip]

Dear:

It was good to see you last week. It's clear that you are enjoying your new job, and I was happy to see that you are so well regarded by the management team at [Company].

I wanted to check back with you concerning the presentation I did on the "open space" concept of subdivisions. I have a PowerPoint slide show that shows the "good" and the "bad" subdivisions and I'd like to present that to the board on my next visit.

I am looking forward to meeting with you and the board again next month. If you have any questions in the interim, please let me know.

Sincerely,

[Name]
[Title]

Letter to Follow Up a Presentation 2

[Date]

[Name]
[Company]
[Address]
[City, State, Zip]

Dear:

I enjoyed meeting your sales staff and appreciate the attentive courtesy shown to me during my presentation: "How to Write an Effective Sales Letter." I have included some samples of letters that address the questions we discussed with your international group.

The list that I have included review the most common "dual-meaning words" between the United States and United Kingdom. I hope this will be helpful.

I will call you next week to discuss the next steps you would like to take to continue this project. Thank you for your interest in our books.

Sincerely,

[Name]
[Title]

Always follow up an in-person presentation. Send the letter to the person with whom you originally set up the presentation. It leaves a good impression and keeps you in mind for the next time they are looking for someone to present this material.

Letter Following Up on Catalog

When you are soliciting business with new potential customers, have a strategic plan for keeping in touch. For instance, send a letter with the catalog you promised, follow up with a phone call in one week, follow up with another letter answering any questions that came up on the phone and perhaps with more literature. Hopefully, the next letter you send will be the cover letter with your contract!

[Date]

[Name]
[Company]
[Address]
[City, State, Zip]

Dear:

Thank you for contacting [Company]. I am following up with you to make sure you received the catalog you requested, and to answer any questions you might have.

The catalog represents our full line of stock products, but please bear in mind we also have the ability to produce stock to your custom specifications.

I will follow up with you next week if I don't hear from you. Please don't hesitate to contact me if you have questions.

Sincerely,

[Name]
[Title]

Letter to Follow Up on a Mailing

[Date]

[Name]
[Company]
[Address]
[City, State, Zip]

Dear:

Recently we sent a mailing to our customers who have purchased [product], inviting you to reorder within the next 30 days at a 10 percent discount.

Time is running out, but if you order by [date], you can still take advantage of the discount and free shipping.

Our customer service representatives are available 24 hours a day to assist you. We look forward to hearing from you.

Sincerely,

[Name]
[Title]

A reminder of a time-sensitive discount with another copy of your catalog may be just the thing needed to get an order.

Part 3

Letters for Sales Operation

Chapter 11

Sales Letters

There are some important factors to consider when writing sales correspondence.

- Check and recheck your letter for accuracy. The different between using the word "can" or "can't" is huge when it comes to outlining credit terms, discounts, etc.

- Identify your potential customer's need and keep that in the forefront. Successful sales letters aren't about what you have to sell, they are about what the letter recipient needs that you just happen to have for sale.

- Never sign off a sales letter without having made it totally clear what the recipient's next step is. Do not expect customers to figure these things out for themselves—you are the one asking for the sale; you need to make purchasing as easy as possible.

Keep your tone conversational but not flip. Parting with money and solving their needs are serious undertakings for most people.

Be Honest

Even though you really want (and perhaps need) to make a sale, do not say anything that you don't know to be absolutely true—shipping time, color choices, use options. Letters put things in writing—the things you want to be able to point to later and the things you perhaps didn't want your customer to point back to. If you don't know something, say so and let the customer know you will find out. And do find out. Letting them know the answer to something you didn't know when you spoke is a great way to get another contact with a follow-up letter, including more literature to keep emphasizing what great products you have.

Being honest may lose you a couple of customers who need to get exactly what they want elsewhere but will go a long way to customer retention. Once people have done business with you and discovered that you care about a true representation of your product or service, they will come back to you for the next need that you can fulfill.

Closing the Sale

Use language in your letter to close the sale. Don't assume just because you are writing a letter and they can't answer right then that you shouldn't ask for the sale. Always ask for the sale.
"How many can I put you down for?" "Should I begin to draft a contract?" These phrases help
place the customer in the purchase mindset, to give them the feeling they would feel if they had
made the purchase. And if it feels ok, they will say yes. But if you don't ask, they have nothing
to answer.

Benefits of Product 1

[Date]

[Name]
[Company]
[Address]
[City, State, Zip]

Dear:

Thank you for your interest in our pressure seal one-piece mailer. Changing to pressure seal is a good way to keep your costs down when changing over from an impact printer to a laser application.

Pressure seal is available in 11- and 14-inch, and in a variety of fold settings. Pressure seal has stock features such as security block-outs, which keep the confidentiality of your message, and can be printed simplex or duplex, so that you can use the maximum amount of "real estate" on your form.

Because the finished piece is a one-piece mailer that meets postal regulations, you can eliminate the need for envelopes or insertions, and, in some cases, can even qualify for postal discounts.

I am including a brochure that lists the features and benefits of this product and would like to work with you to determine if this type of processing is cost-effective for you.

Let me know how many you would like to order!

Sincerely,

[Name]
[Title]

This letter clearly outlines the benefits of the product.

Benefits of Product 2

[Date]

[Name]
[Company]
[Address]
[City, State, Zip]

Dear:

Congratulations on your purchase of the [Name] Coffee Maker. We pride ourselves on manufacturing a quality product and we're sure that you are about to enjoy the best cup of coffee you have ever had.

You can set the timer, set the brew strength, even set the length of time the warmer plate stays on. These features will allow you to make coffee to your specifications and to your lifestyle, eliminating wasted time, and wasted coffee. Our special "as you like it" feature allows you to create 3 different timer settings, so that everyone has their own choice.

Enclosed is a brochure with information on the other fine products we carry. Make a cup of coffee, sit back, and read all about it!

Sincerely,

[Name]
[Title]

Sending a follow up letter after the sale is a great customer relationship builder. There is no pressure—they've already made the purchase. It gives you the opportunity to remind them of key features that they may have forgotten. And keeping you in their minds helps encourage them to recommend your product to their friends.

Benefits of Service 1

[Date]

[Name]
[Company]
[Address]
[City, State, Zip]

Dear:

Home maintenance: Everyone dreads it; everyone knows it has to be done. When you want to spend a warm Saturday afternoon reading a good book with a cold drink, all the chores that you need to do beckon.

By choosing "Take a Break" you have more free time, and rest and relaxation is key to performing your job at 100%. Take a Break can rake your lawn, clean your gutters, mulch your garden. No job is too big, no job is too small, no job is too dirty.

Take a break, and let us help you.

Sincerely,

[Name]
[Title]

This letter clearly lets readers put themselves in a lawn chair and imagine having their chores taken care of while they relax. There's a benefit almost anyone can appreciate!

Benefits of Service 2

This letter describes Corporate Cleaners' regular service and then includes the added benefit of emergency service. Sometimes it is the added benefit that makes the sale.

[Date]

[Name]
[Company]
[Address]
[City, State, Zip]

Dear:

Corporate Cleanup is coming to [City] in [Month]! Our Corporate Cleaners are ready to clean your offices, water and maintain your plants, wash windows, and more.

Image is everything in business, and having customers and prospects visit facilities that are clean, well maintained, and pleasing to the eye goes a long way toward establishing yourself as a company that cares.

Our service means that you never have to worry about drop-in customers, as our weekly cleanup is thorough, and our 2-hour emergency on-site service helps you clean up on short notice.

Let us make you shine!

Sincerely,

[Name]
[Title]

Overcoming Price Objections 1

[Date]

[Name]
[Company]
[Address]
[City, State, Zip]

Dear:

Thank you for your feedback regarding the price quote I sent you. I have reviewed the pricing to see if there were areas where I could reduce your cost, and I have been able to reduce your cost by $.02 per unit. At the overall volume you intend to purchase, the savings are significant.

I realize that you were looking for a reduction that was more than that, and I'd ask you to consider that these units, while slightly higher than your planned budget, are made in the United States, which follows your "made in the USA" mandate. Manufacturing costs are higher here as workers are better trained, and have a higher cost of living commensurate with the overall economy.

Our quality control measures guarantee you that the components you purchase are of the highest quality, durable and safe.

I hope once you take these factors into consideration with the reduction in price, you will choose [Company] as your vendor of choice.

Sincerely,

[Name]
[Title]

If you can reduce costs on a sale, put that right up front in a follow-up letter.

Overcoming Price Objections 2

[Date]

[Name]
[Company]
[Address]
[City, State, Zip]

Dear:

I received your e-mail regarding your pricing questions and I have looked into alternate products that may be less expensive for you.

After researching remanufactured and synthetic products, I still recommend that you use the OEM version of this mode. Original Equipment Manufacture provides you with a guaranteed solution, where remanufactured is "as is" and does have some risk involved.

The small price increase you would absorb by using "OEM" is offset by your ability to return for a full replacement, should any problems occur.

I hope this information is helpful to you.

Sincerely,

[Name]
[Title]

Doing research to help a customer make a decision is a great way to build customer trust and develop a partner-like relationship.

Overcoming Feature Objections 1

[Date]

[Name]
[Company]
[Address]
[City, State, Zip]

Dear:

Thank you for contacting our technical support department regarding the upgraded version of the game, [Name], that was shipped to you.

We have shipped [number] of upgraded game units, and only a handful of customers have found the new scoring system to be inferior to the previous version.

Although we take all customer comments into account, we want to reassure you that the feature you are referring to will allow you to keep score in an interactive format, when you are playing the game with your Internet or cable connection. The "global" scoring feature is especially helpful in league play.

We hope this information helps you better understand the features of the upgrade, and that you continue to enjoy playing [Game name].

Sincerely,

[Name]
[Title]

Don't abandon your customers after the sale is made. Follow up with after-the-sale letters helping customers sort through product features. This is a good way to keep in touch with customers and to let them know you are willing to help them get the most enjoyment and use out of their purchase.

Overcoming Feature Objections 2

[Date]

[Name]

[Company]

[Address]

[City, State, Zip]

Dear:

I appreciate your interest in our product, [Name], and your feedback as an evaluation user. I have looked into your concerns about the high rate of service listed in the MTBF report, and I want to assure you that once users are comfortable with how this equipment works, they are easily trained in the more basic adjustments, and the service call rate decreases significantly.

The data our technical support staff have compiled shows that with the exception of consumable items such as tires, the overall rating for this machine is much higher than average.

Please contact me if you have additional questions.

Sincerely,

[Name]

[Title]

Indicate to customers that you take all feedback seriously and that you don't lose interest in your customers after the sale.

Overcoming Service Objections 1

[Date]

[Name]
[Company]
[Address]
[City, State, Zip]

Dear:

Your letter has been forwarded to my attention as the Manager of the Service Department. I'd like to apologize for the delay in assisting you in your installation needs. Typically, as you know, installation takes place within 7 business days of the purchase.

Your initial call to our service group, on [date], was to request that we not schedule your installation until your return from vacation, the week of [date]. Our technicians were able to honor your request, and your service call was booked in our plan for the week of [date].

I can appreciate that having your vacation cancelled because of weather was frustrating, and that having your installation 2 weeks away was not acceptable to you. However, as my Service Representative explained during the call you made to move out the date, changing your install date effectively moved you to the back of the line.

I have been able to move up the date by 3 business days, but we will not be able to meet your request for an immediate installation, as our crews are booked 72 hours in advance.

I hope this compromise helps you in your planning.

Sincerely,

[Name]
[Title]

Sometimes you just can't overcome a customer's complaint, but compromise when you can.

Overcoming Service Objections 2

[Date]

[Name]
[Company]
[Address]
[City, State, Zip]

Dear:

I appreciate your calling me about the maintenance plan for your software. I hope that I was able to answer your questions. To confirm our talk, software maintenance is mandatory for the first year, and is listed on all price lists and quotes.

We find that during the first year of use, there tend to be more questions that require technical support and training, and maintenance covers these types of calls. Software upgrades are something that is ongoing, for enhanced features as well as fixes for known problems, and again, the maintenance plan assures you that all upgrades are done in a timely manner and at no additional cost.

If you have other questions or concerns please contact me. I hope you find the software to be a valuable tool in creating on-demand forms for your business.

Sincerely,

[Name]
[Title]

Explaining why you require certain things like maintenance lets customers better understand your business practices. Often all it takes is an explanation to avoid a minor frustration turning into a major customer relationship disaster.

Overcoming Poor Past Sales Rep 1

[Date]

[Name]
[Company]
[Address]
[City, State, Zip]

Dear:

I appreciate your taking my call today. I am sorry that the relationship our companies have enjoyed for so many years has been affected by unsatisfactory service from your current account representative.

I have looked into the objections you raised, and while there seems to be circumstances that make these lapses seem less careless than they first appeared, the fact remains that you are not satisfied.

I have assigned [Name] to your account, effective immediately. [Name] is one of our most senior representatives and I think that you will find much in common with [him/her]. If you continue to experience any delays in receiving timely and thorough responses to your questions, please don't hesitate to call me.

Sincerely,

[Name]
[Title]

It is hard to carry on from someone else's bad reputation. Begin to mend fences immediately with a phone call and follow up with a letter reiterating your phone call and outlining exactly what you plan to do change things starting now.

Overcoming Poor Past Sales Rep 2

[Date]

[Name]
[Company]
[Address]
[City, State, Zip]

Dear:

I'm writing to ask you to reconsider canceling your account with us. Your business has been a valuable part of our organization for many years, and losing you is like losing a family member.

You have been quite candid in your criticism of the sales representative handling your account, and you have made clear your feeling that without a change in account management you will not be able to continue to purchase from us.

I don't want to add fuel to the discussion by trying to chalk this up to simply poor compatibility, but I think that you would be more comfortable with a sales representative that is less aggressive. I will make that change effective today.

[Name] will be pleased to manage your account and I would like to stop by with [him/her] next week, so that I can personally introduce [Name] to you.

I hope this is a satisfactory solution for you. I'll call you tomorrow to set up an appointment.

Sincerely,

[Name]
[Title]

A letter is an important one of several steps you will need to take to regain the trust of a customer who is less than satisfied with your business.

Direct Mail Letter 1

[Date]

[Name]
[Company]
[Address]
[City, State, Zip]

Dear:

You have a great product. Your staff is well trained. You have a message. How do you get the message to the customer?

Our direct mail services provide a dynamic mailing piece that will be personalized through interactive mail processing. Each customer receives the same overall piece of information, but imbedded in the piece is a message specific to each recipient.

By selecting key features that the prospect indicates are important, and embedding them into the letter, each letter is personal, without being written individually.

Still skeptical? When you visited our web site, you said the most important thing you needed was "a way to get the message to the customer," and we've used it in your letter, twice!

Let Direct Mail speak for you.

Sincerely,

[Name]
[Title]

In soliciting marketing and direct mail business, be sure to use your own techniques in gaining customers' business.

Direct Mail Letter 2

[Date]

[Name]
[Company]
[Address]
[City, State, Zip]

Dear:

Now that you have visited our web site and looked at our product, I wanted to send you a demo disk so you could try our product.

Install our software, register using the number on the jewel case, and the full power of this home office accounting program will be yours to try for 10 days. This is a risk-free trial, and if you decide to keep the program, call us at the toll-free number on the user manual, and we'll do the rest.

Running a home office isn't easy. Let us automate the accounting functions for you.

Sincerely,

[Name]
[Title]

Acknowledge your potential customer's problem (running a home office isn't easy). It's a good way to let them know you understand their business and know how to help.

Referral Letter 1

[Date]

[Name]
[Company]
[Address]
[City, State, Zip]

Dear:

I have been referred to you by [Name], who spoke highly of your ability to train and motivate an inside sales staff.

[Company] is currently building a sales development and inside sales team, and we are seeking a trainer to provide us with "soup to nuts" sales training.

We want our sales team to understand the importance of identifying the need, handling objections, understanding and communicating features and benefits, and powerful closing.

If you are currently accepting new clients, I'd like to speak with you. If your commitments prevent you from accepting additional opportunities, I would appreciate any referral you would care to make.

I look forward to speaking with you.

Sincerely,

[Name]
[Title]

When looking for team members, tell the prospective candidate just what it was that the referral said that made you think this person is worth contacting and could fit into your business.

Referral Letter 2

[Date]

[Name]
[Company]
[Address]
[City, State, Zip]

Dear:

Thanks for referring me to [Company]. I have been in touch with [Contact] and have provided a proposal and training outline.

I am finishing up a short-term consulting job, and will begin working with their staff the week of [date].

It's always gratifying when a customer feels comfortable offering a recommendation. I appreciate the trust you place in my services through your referrals. I'd like to take you to lunch next week to say thank you. I'll give you a call.

Thanks again.

Sincerely,

[Name]
[Title]

Don't forget to write a thank-you note to those who refer your business or services to other potential customers. This is the best kind of sales lead you can get!

Sales Appreciation Letter 1

[Date]

[Name]
[Company]
[Address]
[City, State, Zip]

Dear:

Thank you for your reorder. I appreciate your continued business and the trust you put in our products. We don't take that confidence for granted, and we are here to provide whatever assistance you need.

I'll be in touch in about six weeks, as that seems to be the reorder cycle for this component, but don't hesitate to contact me any time if you have questions.

Sincerely,

[Name]
[Title]

Reorders are valuable business. Thank them with a note and let customers know you truly value their ongoing business.

Sales Appreciation Letter 2

When you are no longer going to be servicing an account, keep the good relationship going by sending a thank-you note for their business. This helps the next person who will be their representative to start on a positive note. Plus you never know when you are going to run across former contacts in the future. They will remember the last contact they had with you, so let it be a positive one.

[Date]

[Name]
[Company]
[Address]
[City, State, Zip]

Dear:

Thank you for all the courtesy you have extended to me during the past three years. I have enjoyed working with you and while I am excited about my new role in [Company], I will miss the day-to-day interaction with my customers.

I wish you every success for continued good business. Please let me know if I can be of assistance to you in the future. While I leave you in good hands with [New Representative], I will always be available if you need something.

Sincerely,

[Name]
[Title]

Reminder Letter 1

[Date]

[Name]
[Company]
[Address]
(City, State, Zip)

Dear:

It's time to renew your software maintenance! This program assures that you have technical support as well as all product upgrades. We want to make sure that you are able to use this product to its full potential with no interruption in service. Don't delay—you can sign the attached proposal and fax it back to us, or you can send us your company Purchase Order.

Please let me know if you have any questions.

Sincerely,

[Name]
[Title]

Maintenance reminders can also lead to other business. While they are having maintenance done, they might want to investigate replacement of another piece of equipment or upgrading the level of service they currently receive.

Reminder Letter 2

Moving offices can be very disruptive to business. Make a strategic plan to contact customers several times before, during, and after the move to remind them you are still in business and where you can be located. Share your excitement about the changes and invite them to an open house if you plan to have one.

[Date]

[Name]
[Company]
[Address]
[City, State, Zip]

Dear:

We're moving! The big move to our new corporate offices will take place on [dates]. Our distribution center will stop shipping on [date] and our Customer Service and Sales offices will be closed on [date].

Our new phone numbers will be in effect as of [date]. Look for information about our open house in the weeks to come.

Sincerely,

[Name]
[Title]

Chapter 12

Customer Service Letters

Letters to your existing customers are some of the most important letters you will write. The old saying that the satisfied customer will tell one or two other people but the dissatisfied customer will tell a dozen or more people about their bad experience is very true. Well-crafted and timely letters will help your customers think positively about your business. Some of the most egregious mistakes can be smoothed over with a good letter from the appropriate person at the company. Sending letters to your customers is simply a great way to build a relationship with the people who are critical to your business.

Still Keep It Short

Letters to your customers, particularly those responding to complaints, can be a little longer than unsolicited sales letters. But don't go on forever. If the key information in your helpful response to a customer's complaint is buried in several paragraphs, your customer won't get to the useful information before they throw the letter away anyway.

Different Kinds of Letters

There are several different types of customer service letter:

- Confirmation letters confirm information that you and the customer have exchanged, such as delivery date and time of a product or service, date of a meeting, or a cover letter with a contract that confirms the customer's order.

- Thank you letters never go out of fashion—send them and send them often. Thank customers for outstanding loyalty, for trying your business for the first time, for recommending you to their friends and family.

- Follow-up letters are a great way to prove to customers that you do what you say you will. If you promised to get them some information or to send a brochure or to give them a quote, do it. And follow up with a letter. You will follow up with a phone call too, but letters are a great way to keep a paper trail of your contacts, and to give people time to think about things before having to talk on the phone.

Surveys

Customer feedback is critical to successful sales. Sending a survey following a purchase or service is a great way to get some useful feedback. And most customers like to feel that you care enough about their satisfaction to solicit their feedback.

Keep surveys short and simple but be sure to ask about the key things you are interested in. Offer a gift certificate or discount coupon for returning the survey as an incentive for the customer to use their valuable time to help you be more effective. And point out all of these things in a brief cover letter.

Discount Schedule 1

[Date]

[Name]
[Company]
[Address]
[City, State, Zip]

Dear:

We are pleased to announce a change in our discount schedule, which we feel will be a benefit to all our clients.

Effective [date], our discount schedule will be separate for parts and labor so that customers who are only purchasing one service or the other will still be able to take advantage of a discount.

We hope these changes, which are the result of customer feedback, are helpful to you.

Sincerely,

[Name]
[Title]

Changes in discount schedule, especially those that favor the customer, are clearly worth sending out an informational letter about. Be clear about the change and how it is better than the previous discount schedule.

Discount Schedule 2

[Date]

[Name]
[Company]
[Address]
[City, State, Zip]

Dear:

We're pleased to announce that our newest printer will be available for purchase this month. This MFP (multi-function printer) offers the latest in printing, copying, scanning, and uploading documents for archiving.

As a part of our introductory offer, companies that pre-buy, or set up their lease before [date] will be eligible for an additional 10% discount. This offer cannot be combined with any other discount offer. Discount is on the base price; accessories, taxes, etc. are not included.

We hope you will take advantage of our offer.

Sincerely,

[Name]
[Title]

A mass mailing of a special such as this to all your existing customers and to lists you purchase can provide some good sales leads.

Changes to Discount Schedule

[Date]

[Name]
[Company]
[Address]
[City, State, Zip]

Dear:

At our quarterly sales meeting, there was a discussion concerning price breaks at the lower quantities. We have researched our orders for the past year for [products], and the current discounts we are offering at the 10-case and below prices are not enticing customers to look at the higher quantities.

We would like to get your feedback on how the discount structure works in your territory. Please contact your sales manager to discuss this before the end of the month.

Sincerely,

[Name]
[Title]

Salespeople out in the field can provide great input into how customers might react to a new offering. Be sure to point out exactly who they should give the results of their research to.

Credit Terms 1

[Date]

[Name]
[Company]
[Address]
[City, State, Zip]

Dear:

Thank you for your interest in reselling our products. Our accounting department has completed its processing, and I am pleased to tell you that you are now able to order on terms, with the presentation of a hard copy purchase order.

Our terms are 2% 5, net 45, and we accept payment by check, or electronically. Payments that are made by credit card are not eligible for discount.

Your sales representative is [Name] and [he/she] will be in touch to go over our purchasing requirements and answer any questions you might have.

Welcome to our family of resellers!

Sincerely,

[Name]
[Title]

Resellers represent your company and you should be sure to provide them with everything they need to do that in the way you want your company represented.

Credit Terms 2

[Date]

[Name]
[Company]
[Address]
[City, State, Zip]

Dear:

Thank you for your recent order. We have noted that the terms on your purchase order state 2% 10, net 30, whereas our terms, as noted on quote #23837, list our standard terms as 1% 10, net 30.

Please confirm that you will honor our stated terms, so that we can process your order.

Sincerely,

[Name]
[Title]

Although a conflict such as this might first be dealt with over the phone, it is important to have verification in writing. Be sure not to be accusatory or indicate they are trying to "get away with something." Simply state the facts and take it from there.

Change in Service 1

[Date]

[Name]
[Company]
[Address]
[City, State, Zip]

Dear:

Thank you for your call today. This is to confirm your request for a change in your service plan, from on-site next-day service to on-site same-day service.

Same-day service means that a technician will contact you by telephone within four hours of your service call to determine the problem. Generally issues will be corrected by a technical support call. Should an on-site visit be required, you will be scheduled within four hours, provided it is before the end of the normal business day (5 p.m. in the time zone of the customer). If the call comes in after 1:00 p.m., customer time, then service will be the first call of the next business day.

We have included an updated contract, which details the terms of service, and on receipt of your signed copy, will invoice you based on the new service plan. We appreciate your business, and look forward to working with you on a continuing basis.

Sincerely,

[Name]
[Title]

A written letter outlining changes in service is an important way to have any changes documented and allows the customer to see in writing what they have ordered.

Change in Service 2

[Date]

[Name]
[Company]
[Address]
[City, State, Zip]

Dear:

We are pleased to announce that [Company] has entered into an agreement with [Name] for field support of all our computer hardware.

[New Company] has the advantage of service representatives in every state, as well as contracts with local hardware technicians in the more remote locations. This will give us a better response time, and will ultimately improve the manner of service you receive.

While this change is significant for us, you will not see a change in the cost of your service plan in the foreseeable future. We urge you to provide us with both positive and negative feedback on your experience in the coming months, so that we can make any changes as we renew our contract at the end of the year.

Thank you for your continued business.

Sincerely,

[Name]
[Title]

Announcement of partnerships with another company is a great chance to send out a letter to existing customers. Be sure to point out the positive ways that the partnership impacts the customer's relationship with the company.

Change of Address 1

[Date]

[Name]
[Company]
[Address]
[City, State, Zip]

Dear:

We are pleased to announce that the construction of our new manufacturing and corporate offices has been completed, and we will be moving to our new "home" effective [date].

Our telephone, fax, and e-mail information is exactly the same. Please note our billing lock box address is also the same, but our physical address is as follows:

[Detail]

We are excited that this long-awaited move is complete and we look forward to being able to provide expanded services to our clients as we continue to grow.

Sincerely,

[Name]
[Title]

Moving your business is a major change and customers need to be kept apprised.

Change of Address 2

[Date]

[Name]
[Company]
[Address]
[City, State, Zip]

Dear:

This is to inform all our customers who currently utilize service under the "depot return" plan that our depot service address has changed, effective immediately.

Depot service returns should now be sent to the following address:

[Detail]

Please contact your customer service representative if you have any questions.

Sincerely,

[Name]
[Title]

Notification of changes of address should be sent immediately to all customers. All invoices and other written correspondence from there on for up to a year should have the change of address pointed out.

Confirmation Letter 1

This letter outlines a very important point about checking the order before the items are manufactured. Having this kind of thing in writing helps in the event that the product manufactured is not what the customer thought he or she ordered.

[Date]

[Name]
[Company]
[Address]
[City, State, Zip]

Dear:

Thank you for your order. An order confirmation is attached for your records. Please check it carefully as the specifications noted are exactly what the plant will produce. You will receive a proof within 4 business days that you will need to sign to approve, or, if changes are needed, note changes requested and send the proof back to our office.

Your sales representative is [Name]. Please don't hesitate to call [him/her] if you have any questions.

Sincerely,

[Name]
[Title]

Confirmation Letter 2

[Date]

[Name]
[Company]
[Address]
[City, State, Zip]

Dear:

Thanks for your time on the phone today. This is to confirm our meeting, scheduled for [date and time]. I will bring the samples you requested and we can look at the plans you have drawn up to this point, as a precursor to an actual quote for service.

If you have any questions before the meeting, please contact me. I look forward to meeting you in person.

Sincerely,

[Name]
[Title]

Customers appreciate confirmation of any meetings you arranged and what the purpose of the meeting is. The onus is on you as the salesperson to remind customers of the scheduled meeting and a letter is a great way to do it.

Letter Relating to Contracts 1

A letter like this that seems to come out of the blue can really impress customers. Even though it relates to selling (a continuation of their service plan, in this case), a letter like this makes it seem like they are actually on your mind other than when they call wanting to buy something.

[Date]

[Name]
[Company]
[Address]
[City, State, Zip]

Dear:

The service plan you purchased for your central air conditioning is due to expire on [date]. We hope that you found our service technicians to be knowledgeable and courteous and that you are satisfied.

A renewal contract is included with this letter, and we encourage you to consider continuing your service plan. Routine, regular maintenance has proven to increase the life and efficiency of equipment like this, and with the summer approaching, having your air conditioning in top operating condition is the best way to keep customers and employees happy!

Please contact our office if you have any questions, or would like to change the terms of your service plan.

Sincerely,

[Name]
[Title]

Letter Relating to Contracts 2

[Date]

[Name]
[Company]
[Address]
[City, State, Zip]

Dear:

Thank you for your proposal, which outlines your services as an on-site consultant to our Sales Management team for a 12-week period. I have reviewed the scope of service and have forwarded it to our legal department and we are ready to sign off and retain your services.

A standard consultant contract is attached, as well as a confidentiality agreement. We are in the final stages of Research and Development for a new product launch, and would like to have you involved in that from a sales perspective.

If you have any questions regarding the contract for confidentiality clause, please call our Corporate Attorney at [number]. We look forward to formalizing our agreement.

Sincerely,

[Name]
[Title]

Contracts are important sales tools. Be sure to outline any important details—such as the confidentiality agreement and the length of the contract—in a letter so the recipient doesn't overlook these key items.

Letter Responding to Complaint 1

[Date]

[Name]
[Company]
[Address]
[City, State, Zip]

Dear:

I am writing in response to your posting on our Customer Service web site and your complaint regarding the quality of your [Brand] boots.

Our company takes great pride in manufacturing a quality product, but as with any product that is handmade, mistakes can and do occur. Had you contacted the dealer where you made your initial purchase, you would have been instructed to return the product to them, so that they could replace your boots and return the defective pair to us.

Since you prefer not to go to the retailer where you made the initial purchase, please return your boots to us, at the address listed on the attached RMA (return materials authorization.) Our quality control department will inspect them, and should a defect be found that is the result of a manufacturing error, they will be replaced at no charge.

If, for some reason, our inspectors feel that the issue is due to abuse or consumer neglect, the product will be returned to you with an explanatory note.

Please contact our office if you have any questions.

Sincerely,

[Name]
[Title]

Returns and customer dissatisfaction are part of life as a salesperson. Stand behind your product while sticking to your return policies.

Letter Responding to Complaint 2

to [Date]

[Name]
[Company]
[Address]
[City, State, Zip]

Dear:

I'm following up on the telephone conversation we had yesterday regarding your dissatisfaction with our policy of requiring full company information, before we provide you with a price quote.

The products and services we offer are considered secure documents, and as such, we need to assure that we are dealing with a reputable, registered business before we discuss pricing and shipping options.

This policy is not designed to imply that a caller is less than reputable; rather, it is in place to assure that the dealers we ship to are qualified, and therefore to protect all resellers through this diligence.

I hope this information helps assure you that our goal is to protect all customers equally,

Sincerely,

[Name]
[Title]

Customer complaints, like returns, are a part of sales life. A phone call where warranted, followed up by a simple written explanation about policies while being respectful of the customer's complaint is the best way to deal with it.

Letter Regarding Shipping and Handling Issues 1

[Date]

[Name]
[Company]
[Address]
[City, State, Zip]

Dear:

Thank you for your letter dated [date], and your inquiry regarding shipping and handling. We have relationships with all the major shipping companies and have special pricing contracts with them. We pass these discounts on to you directly so that you may also take advantage of these savings.

When no specific carrier is requested on a purchase order, our shipping department selects the most economic means of ground transportation, typically UPS. We are happy to honor any requests you have, and we can ship billing to your account, if you request it.

Please let your sales representative know if you have any preferences and we will work within those guidelines.

I hope this answers your questions, but don't hesitate to contact me if you need more information.

Sincerely,

[Name]
[Title]

Putting information like shipping and handling policies in writing can take care of any possible confusion that comes up later.

Letter Regarding Shipping and Handling Issues 2

[Date]

[Name]
[Company]
[Address]
[City, State, Zip]

Dear:

I appreciate your telephone call and have looked into the shipping charges for your order number [PO number]. Our customer service department provided you with an estimate of freight charges, as noted in their e-mail to you dated [date]. A copy of that correspondence is attached. We are happy to provide our customers with an estimate, but an estimate is not a guaranteed freight cost, as noted.

Fluctuations in fuel charges have caused many of our vendors to add on a surcharge to cover these day-to-day changes in the cost of transportation, and while we pass on our discounts to our customers, we are also bearing the burden of these rate increases.

We will do our best to estimate freight as you request. I hope this information is helpful to you.

Sincerely,

[Name]
[Title]

Shipping charges are often something a salesperson has to deal with before the sale is made. Explanations of the company's logic behind their shipping charges can help deflate customer concerns.

Thank-You Letter 1

[Date]

[Name]
[Company]
[Address]
[City, State, Zip]

Dear:

I have received your fax and processed your reorder for immediate shipment. I want to take this opportunity to thank you for your business. Your trust and continued support of our products through your purchase is important to us. On behalf of everyone here at [Company], I want to say thank you.

Your order will ship this week and tracking will be sent to you automatically. Thank you, again, for your order.

Sincerely,

[Name]
[Title]

Loyal customers can never be thanked enough for their ongoing business.

Thank-You Letter 2

[Date]

[Name]
[Company]
[Address]
[City, State, Zip]

Dear:

Thank you for taking the time to meet with me yesterday. I hope that the product demonstration answered your questions, and that you will view our product favorably when making your decision.

The pricing that I left with you is valid for 30 days. These products are in stock for immediate shipment, and I look forward to your order.

If you have any additional questions as you continue to evaluate the product, please give me a call. Thanks again.

Sincerely,

[Name]
[Title]

Demonstrations can be a key component of sales depending on your product. Always follow up a demo with a letter. Tempt potential buyers with dated pricing and remind them that the product can be theirs almost immediately.

Credit and Collection Letter: Soft

[Date]

[Name]
[Company]
[Address]
[City, State, Zip]

Dear:

Thank you for your time yesterday. I am including with this letter the invoices that I show as open. I would appreciate your reviewing them with you Accounts Payable staff, so that we can determine when these were paid. I will have our AR Manager go through our records based on your check number and date paid.

If you need additional information, please let me know.

Sincerely,

[Name]
[Title]

Keep tabs on overdue accounts and send credit and collections letters promptly. The longer a bill is overdue, the less likely you are to get paid.

Credit and Collection Letter: Final

[Date]

[Name]
[Company]
[Address]
[City, State, Zip]

Dear:

I have contacted you several times in the past 90 days regarding your unpaid invoice in the amount of $[amount], with no reply. Frankly, I'm baffled. Our company extended a line of credit to you on terms, based on an agreement that you would pay for your purchases within those terms.

We cannot continue to work with you if you don't respond to our inquiries. Regretfully, unless we hear from you within 5 business days, we will turn this matter over to our attorneys. We are willing to accept a payment plan, but you will need to contact us immediately. Once this has been given to our legal department, we cannot accept any payment other than in full, with any legal or collection fees we have incurred.

We regret sending this letter, but your silence has given us no choice.

Regretfully,

[Name]
[Title]

Give customers with overdue accounts every option for paying—several notices, payment terms, etc. Then make it clear that you will immediately begin to use all the resources at your disposal to collect.

Letter Seeking Feedback on Product 1

Customer feedback is valuable to your sales efforts. Solicit it often through phone calls, written surveys, and postcards included with products or left with the customer after services are rendered.

[Date]

[Name]
[Company]
[Address]
[City, State, Zip]

Dear:

Thank you for your order dated [date]. We are pleased you selected [Company] to provide you with [product] and hope that you have been satisfied to date.

We randomly select customers who have ordered for the first time, and send them an evaluation form, so that we can gauge the overall satisfaction with our product as well as learn how it is being used in the market.

If you could take a few moments to fill out the enclosed survey, and return it in the postage paid envelope provided, it will help us continue to offer the highest quality products that it is possible to manufacture.

Your assistance is appreciated.

Sincerely,

[Name]
[Title]

Letter Seeking Feedback on Product 2

[Date]

[Name]
[Company]
[Address]
[City, State, Zip]

Dear:

Our records show that you had returned your original lawnmower to us, as defective, and it was replaced with a new unit on [date]. We are sorry that your initial experience with us was not satisfactory.

We take great pride in producing a top-quality product, but occasionally mistakes do occur. The purpose of this letter is to seek your input on how the replacement product has worked for you.

Please fill out the enclosed post card and send it to us at your convenience. We hope you will accept the enclosed gift certificate with our apologies for the inconvenience and our thanks.

Sincerely,

[Name]
[Title]

Extra measures should be taken when a customer returns a defective product. In this case, being unafraid to request feedback and including a gift certificate show that you stand by your products and care about customer satisfaction.

Letter Seeking Feedback on Service 1

Service providers constantly seek customer feedback in order to provide better service. Customers will reveal small things you can do to make their experience a better one—one that they will refer to their friends and family. Happy customers mean more sales!

[Date]

[Name]
[Company]
[Address]
[City, State, Zip]

Dear:

Thank you for choosing [Name] as the service provider for your vehicle. We have been servicing cars and trucks since [year] and our service technicians are factory trained and certified.

I am the Service Manager for [Company], and I hope that your first experience with us was a positive one. I am enclosing a survey, which gives you the chance to rate our service in 5 key areas. I hope you will take a moment and fill it out, and drop it in the mail to my attention. Once we have your response, we will send you a coupon good for a free fluids check, the next time you bring your vehicle in for service.

Thank you for your attention, and your business.

Sincerely,

[Name]
[Title]

Letter Seeking Feedback on Service 2

[Date]

[Name]
[Company]
[Address]
[City, State, Zip]

Dear:

Thank you for allowing us to visit your home and provide a complete steam clean and restoration of your carpets. Your business is appreciated and we value your feedback.

It is important to our company that our service staff is knowledgeable, courteous, and efficient in their service to you. In order to assure that we are training our home care staff in all aspects of customer service, it would be helpful if you could complete the enclosed response card and send it to us, with our thanks.

Please don't hesitate to contact me personally, if you have any questions.

Sincerely,

[Name]
[Title]

When you send response cards, be sure they are self-addressed and stamped. Also point out to customers that you are looking to ensure that they are getting everything they want for their money and that your service meets their expectations. This feedback is particularly important for services that happen regularly, like vehicle oil changes or weekly house-cleaning service.

Letter Seeking Feedback on Customer Service 1

Web sites are a great way to get fast customer feedback. Although some customers won't have access to the Internet, that is quickly becoming the exception not the rule.

[Date]

[Name]
[Company]
[Address]
[City, State, Zip]

Dear:

Our records show that you contacted our customer service representatives on [date] with questions about [product].

One of the most important things we do is treat our customers with the care and respect they deserve. Would you take a moment to give us feedback on your experience?

Please visit our web site, [www.ww.com], and click on the link to customer service feedback.

Thank you for your interest in our products. We hope to hear from you again!

Sincerely,

[Name]
[Title]

Letter Seeking Feedback on Customer Service 2

[Date]

[Name]
[Company]
[Address]
[City, State, Zip]

Dear:

[Company name] considers customer service to be the key component of our mission statement. We regard your customer service experience as encompassing everything from the ease in which you navigated our web site, to how the package was shipped.

We ask that you take a few minutes and fill out the enclosed survey. It gives you the chance to let us know how we did, from beginning to end, and gives us the chance to make improvements based on customer input.

Please accept the enclosed gift certificate, with our thanks in advance for your participation.

Sincerely,

[Name]
[Title]

Survey requests often include an incentive like a gift certificate.

Chapter 13

Letters, E-mails, and Memos for Sales Management

The sales manager position is critical for support and success of the sales force. A sales manager should manage—use meetings of course, but in between individual and group sales meetings, back up your management with letters, e-mails, and memos that keep salespeople in the loop about anything they need to know.

Content

What should be in written correspondence to sales staff? Just about everything. Your salespeople need to know anything that has an impact on their ability to be out in the field (or on the phone) selling. They can't be promising shipping turnaround times or discount schedules only to find out that these details were altered two months ago and no one bothered to spread the word.

Letters

Letters are the medium of choice for personnel issues. Anything regarding congratulating, praising, or reprimanding an employee should be done in person and then followed up in writing in a formal letter on company letterhead with the manager's signature. This gives the employee the opportunity to include this in their personal portfolio, in the case of praise. When performance issues or actual reprimands are being covered, a letter gives you written documentation to include in the employee's file in the event that the issue does not get resolved.

Letters are also the preferred method of communication in most customer-related issues. Memos are too informal and should be reserved for announcements; e-mails are just too fleeting and have too many opportunities to get in the wrong hands.

Memos

Memos, i.e., memorandums, are especially useful for in-house announcements. They can be printed and tucked in each employee's mailbox and they can be posted on bulletin boards. Use a memo to announce company policy changes like dress code, employee discounts, the details of the company holiday party or summer outing. Memos are informal, casual, and good for inside the company.

E-mail

You are going to use e-mail a lot. There is no way around it in the current communications climate. But despite how easy and fast e-mail seems, be careful about using e-mail for important or confidential correspondence. There is nothing confidential about e-mail—not even counting the fact that it is so easy to input the wrong person in the "To" line or press the "Reply to All" button on an e-mail to multiple people when there was really only one person you wanted to see your reply. Use e-mail often—for verifying information, setting up appointments, checking in to keep in touch—but use letters for anything important.

Promotion Letter

[Date]

[Name]
[Company]
[Address]
[City, State, Zip]

Dear:

It is our pleasure to confirm that you have been promoted to the challenging and demanding position of [position].

We are confident that you will meet the new responsibilities that accompany the position with the same level of enthusiasm and enterprise that you have exhibited. We know that you will bring new perspective to this opportunity.

Please accept our congratulations on your new promotion.

Sincerely,

[Name]
[Title]

You will also want to create a memorandum to distribute this promotion to the company, and perhaps use e-mail as well. But the formal letter gives the employee an important piece of correspondence to add to his or her portfolio.

Job Offer Letter 1

[Date]

[Name]
[Company]
[Address]
[City, State, Zip]

Dear:

We are pleased to confirm your employment by our firm. You will report directly to [Name], commencing with your start of employment on [start date].

If you agree that the attached letter detailing the terms of your employment agrees with your understanding, please sign the enclosed copy and return for our files.

We look forward to your joining the company.

Sincerely,

[Name]
[Title]

Appointments should definitely come in the form of a letter. You will almost certainly have already talked with the new hire by phone to give her or him the news, but a follow-up letter is a must.

Job Offer Letter 2

Send job offer letters as soon as possible. If the employment contract can't accompany it, then send the letter out on its own and indicate the contract will follow. This is the place where prospective employees will see exactly what your company culture is like. Also, you want to be sure they are on board and don't change their minds—the hiring process is long, involved, and costly.

[Date]

[Name]
[Company]
[Address]
[City, State, Zip]

Dear:

On behalf of the Management Team and the Board of Directors, it is my pleasure to welcome you to our organization.

We look forward to your joining us on [date]. Information regarding the specifics of your employment will be forwarded to you under separate cover.

Sincerely,

[Name]
[Title]

Job Performance

[Date]

[Name]
[Company]
[Address]
[City, State, Zip]

Dear:

Despite an earlier oral warning I feel it is necessary to provide you with written notification that your employment with [Company] could be in jeopardy.

As an employee and as part of your contract of employment you are responsible for working a 40-hour week, Monday through Friday, from 8:30 a.m. to 5:00 p.m.

This firm employed you because we were impressed not only by your skills and experience but by the impression you made when you joined us. Clearly, you have talent and the potential to do well in this company.

Teamwork is essential if a company is to work well. Teamwork requires each of us giving 100%, so that we can achieve all the department's targets and objectives.

If you are having problems that are causing you difficulty, please come and see me. If not, from this date I look forward to a marked improvement in your attendance, not only for the sake of the company but also for your own.

Sincerely,

[Name]
[Title]

Performance warnings definitely need to be in writing in a formal letter. If you need to follow through with termination of employment, you will need written documentation to back you up.

Performance Review 1

[Date]

[Name]
[Company]
[Address]
[City, State, Zip]

Dear:

It was a pleasure meeting with you regarding your performance with us during [time-frame]. We appreciate your commitment to improve on the areas we identified.

Enclosed you will find a copy of the performance evaluation we reviewed on [date]. This copy is for your records, with the original retained in your personnel file.

Please don't hesitate to speak with your manager, or myself, if you find it difficult to meet the objectives we've outlined. We want you to succeed and we are confident that you can overcome your recent performance issues and exceed our expectations.

Sincerely,

[Name]
[Title]

Annual evaluation time is also a good place for a letter. Don't cheat your employees—be very professional when it comes to employment and performance issues, good and bad.

Performance Review 2

[Date]

[Name]
[Company]
[Address]
[City, State, Zip]

Dear:

Congratulations on your outstanding performance review for the past year! We are gratified at the consistent level of effort you have put into a very difficult position. Your career with us is just beginning, but with continued hard work, we are certain that you will achieve great success with our organization.

Your formal review, which you were given on [date], has been signed and is now on record in your personnel file. The attached copy is for your records.

Congratulations, again, on a job well done!

Sincerely,

[Name]
[Title]

A good performance is always a great chance for a letter that the employee can add to a personal portfolio.

Memo to Sales Manager: Setting Goals 1

To:
Fr:
Re:
Date:

Your sales managers should help you set goals and obtain them. Solicit their help regularly.

I'd like to set up a meeting with you sometime this week to discuss my goals for the coming year. I have reviewed my sales year to date and created a forecast for projected sales for the next 2 quarters, and I would like to discuss this with you.

In addition, I would like to request additional leads for my territory, as I feel I have addressed the time management concerns you expressed at my 6-month review.

I look forward to our meeting.

Memo to Sales Manager: Setting Goals 2

To:

Fr:

Re:

Date:

As you requested I am attaching my sales report for the preceding 3 quarters and my anticipated sales for the 4th quarter. I would like to meet with you at your earliest convenience to discuss my goal for the coming year.

Sales reps need to keep their managers apprised of their efforts regularly.

Memo to Sales Manager: Adjusting Goals 1

Goals are just that—goals. Sometimes you meet them, sometimes you exceed them, sometimes factors step in that prevent you from meeting them. A memo to your manager should keep him or apprised as to where you are.

To:

Fr:

Re:

Date:

I would like to schedule a meeting with you this week to discuss adjusting my goal. As you know, the first 2 quarters of the year I was in sales part-time, with half of my time spent in credit/collections.

Although I am now in sales full-time, I still have the responsibility of managing all computer hardware upgrades, which takes about 3 hours per week. Because my performance evaluation is based on achieving an annual sales goal, I would like to discuss the possibility of pro-rating my sales goal based on how much time I was given to perform sales each quarter.

I have attached some customer and sales reports for your review prior to our meeting. Please let me know if you can accommodate my request.

Memo to Sales Manager: Adjusting Goals 2

To:
Fr:
Re:
Date:

I have attached a report of current open proposals for my territory, in response to your memo concerning adjusting sales goals. I have provided this information on an Excel Spreadsheet, so that you can view the information by any one of the column headers.

Please let me know if you need additional information.

Being a salesperson involves generating lots of reports. Help your sales manager keep the corporate office happy with the information they need to regularly update projections.

Memo to Sales Manager: Reporting Activities 1

Let managers know how your sales reports are organized so they don't start off reading them the wrong way!

To:
Fr:
Re:
Date:

Attached you will find the activity report for my sales team for the previous month. I have grouped them by sales representative, and within that group, have further sorted them in descending order by sales value.

Please let me know if you would like to meet with me and go over the information.

Memo to Sales Manager: Reporting Activities 2

To:
Fr:
Re
Date:

Thank you for your call. I am including my activity report for each week of the previous two quarters. The activities are listed as follows:

- Cold calls
- Appointments generated from inside sales
- Appointments generated from cold calls
- Courtesy calls to existing customers
- Troubleshooting/inventory calls

I hope this information helps you in your data collection. Let me know if you need anything else at this time.

Itemizing your sales reports will indicate to your manager where you are spending your time. A good manager will help you determine if your choices are successful and recommend changes that might help.

Memo to Sales Manager: Reporting Results 1

To:

Fr:

Re:

Date:

Attached you will find reports for each individual sales representative and for the team as a whole, for the previous month. I have noted the following:

- Cold calls that resulted in an appointment
- Appointments that resulted in a sale
- Repeat orders from existing customers

My team is on track for the month, and we have projected sales for next month that will keep us on target.

Let me know if you have any questions.

Using the word "results" in a memo about sales is key—results are what the readers of sales reports and memos are looking for.

Memo to Sales Manager: Reporting Results 2

To:
Fr:
Re:
Date:

I have the results of the fax-back campaign that our group did last month on the new hardware for Call Centers. The complete report is attached, but here are the highlights of interest:

Number of customers contacted in fax-back program: 175

Number of customers who responded without call: 12

Number of customers who responded after call: 25

This is a 21% participation rate after 2 weeks. Please let me know if you have any questions once you review the data.

Numbers are key in the sales world. Try to always include some in reports and memos about sales activities.

Memo to Sales Manager: Addressing Problem with Customer 1

To:
Fr:
Re:
Date:

Keep sales managers apprised of customer dissatisfaction and head it off. Tell them your side of the story before the customer does.

I want to bring to your attention an issue we have had with [Customer name]. As you know, in the past there have been several instances where this customer, when calling in and noting their regular sales rep unavailable, has been verbally abusive to the person answering the phone. Recently, when [Name] called and learned their sales representative was on another call, [Name] again became abusive, insisting that the other customer could be called back so that his needs could be attended to immediately.

I have called [Name] and it was clear to me after only a brief conversation that the abuse has been, if anything, understated. I have offered [Name] an option to continue to do business with our organization by fax or e-mail only, or, regretfully we must discontinue servicing him as our customer.

I want to bring to your attention the professionalism and courtesy that our staff showed [Name], even in the face of yelling and name-calling. They are to be commended.

Memo to Sales Manager: Addressing Problem with Customer 2

To:
Fr:
Re:
Date:

I want to bring to your attention a customer order error, which could have resulted in a large and costly problem for our company, which was averted thanks to our Customer Service Staff.

The order for [Customer] was due to ship on Friday. [Name] in our customer service group was getting the commercial invoice ready to accompany the packing list, and noticed that the number of cartons on the packing list was not correct. This was due to a stock change, and the new item has larger quantities per case.

[Name] corrected the paperwork, adjusted the commercial invoice to reflect the way the product was packaged, and the order proceeded without incident.

Had this attention to detail been lacking, the order would have been held up at customs, and would have resulted in delays as well as additional duties and taxes.

Our Sales Organization places a huge burden on Customer Service to get the orders right, and [Name] should be singled out for special recognition as part of a great team.

> Give praise where praise is due. Employees appreciate it.

Memo to Sales Manager: Customer's Payment Problem 1

Use a memo to point out to your supervisors that you can handle situations with your customers. It will prove useful in the future.

To:

Fr:

Re:

Date:

As you had requested I telephoned [Customer name] to discuss their outstanding invoice. The problem is apparently two-fold. The company has implemented new Accounts Payable Software, and it was recently discovered that because of a user error, several accounts were overlooked for payment. Compounding the problem is that the AP Supervisor has been on medical leave, so the audits did not catch the discrepancy.

A check for the full amount will be cut on Tuesday, and sent by overnight mail. Thank you for letting me resolve this situation with my customer.

Memo to Sales Manager: Customer's Payment Problem 2

To:
Fr:
Re:
Date:

I have been in contact with [Company] regarding the outstanding invoices for product. I was given the impression that there is a serious financial issue. Nothing was said to me directly, but my contact implied that there was to be an announcement in the next week about the future of the company as a whole.

I was not able to gain a commitment for payment, even on a program basis. I suggest that we take whatever legal steps would be appropriate, so that if the company files for bankruptcy protection, we are listed as waiting for payment.

Part of being in sales is dealing with delinquent accounts. Keep the company fully aware of problems as they arise.

Memo to Sales Manager: Problem with Fellow Employee 1

Personnel issues can take up a lot of time of any manager, sales being no exception. Put all personnel issues in writing.

To:
Fr:
Re:
Date:

I wish to advise you that I have met with [Name] and [Name] individually and together, to address the friction between them and try to resolve these issues without losing either employee.

Individually, their concerns were almost identical. Each is annoyed by a personal habit of the other, and they had let it get to a point where they weren't able to talk about it to one another.

I met with them together, and had each one repeat their issue, to me, with their associate listening quietly. Once they had both aired their views, they began to see the humor in the situation, and were more inclined to work their problems out with one another. At this juncture I felt that it would be better if I left the room for a few minutes so they could speak frankly, since it was apparent the friction had eased. On my return, they both apologized to me, and to one another, and I feel the situation has been corrected.

One note of interest came out of the meeting, and that is they both feel that their particular quarters are much smaller than all the other "rows." We measured their workspace and compared it to the row adjacent to them and in fact they have the same workspace area as other employees but the aisle between them is only 2/3 as wide as all the other corridors. This very likely adds to their feeling of no privacy, and I think we should have maintenance address that by moving partitions so that they have the same space as other workers.

I have advised each employee that this was an informal meeting, and provided no additional issues occurred it would not be necessary to put a note in their employment record.

Memo to Sales Manager: Problem with Fellow Employee 2

To:

Fr:

Re:

Date:

I have met with [Name] and discussed the atmosphere between us, and made an effort to offer some corrective action measure that I think will ease the situation.

It is apparent to me, now that we have spoken, that the problem I have been experiencing goes beyond a misunderstanding, and I am not hopeful that the suggestions I made to lighten the mood in our area will be considered.

I would ask that you spend some time in our area in the next few days, discreetly if possible, and meet with each of us, as individuals and together. Perhaps with your input we can gain a mutual accord.

Peace among personnel is an elusive but admirable goal and should be pursued at all times.

Memo to Sales Manager: Reporting Success 1

Keep your sales manager apprised on all customer-related issues and how they were resolved.

To:

Fr:

Re:

Date:

I wanted to follow up with you regarding the ongoing installation issue we've had with [Customer's] software upgrade. I have been working with Technical Support all week to determine why the output will not print to the networked laser printer, and we are pleased to report we have resolved the problem.

Apparently at one point the networked printer for this area was another model entirely, and there were still some driver files imbedded on the PC that were causing a print error.

The customer is now able to successfully print, and is very pleased with our efforts.

Memo to Sales Manager: Reporting Success 2

To:

Fr:

Re:

Date:

Our Sales Goals for the month have been achieved, and I am attaching the individual sales totals for your review. My staff worked very hard, and spent long hours in the past 2 weeks to assure that all proposals were reviewed, closed, or converted to sale.

We also have 2 contest winners based on sales of the new office equipment. Invoice copies are attached.

Keep sales competitions in the forefront with memos announcing results.

Memo to Sales Manager: Addressing a Compensation Issue 1

To:

Fr:

Re:

Date:

Keep employees happy by rewarding performance.

I would like to meet with you at your earliest opportunity to discuss increasing the base compensation for [Name]. Although [he/she] has been with the company less than one year, the revenue that [he/she] has brought to the organization is significant. The fact that we have hired an experienced sales representative has decreased the learning curve and should be rewarded.

Please let me know when you are available to discuss this.

Memo to Sales Manager: Addressing a Compensation Issue 2

To:
Fr:
Re:
Date:

I am attaching a list of those staff members who are eligible for a payroll increase. I would like to meet with you to review their work history and discuss possible salary increases. Please let me know when it is convenient for you to meet with me.

It often takes continual effort and reminding to keep corporate directors on task when it comes to employee salary increases.

Memo to Sales Manager: Eliciting Support for an Idea 1

It is a rare company that doesn't value employee suggestions for doing things more efficiently and effectively. Memos are a good way to outline an idea—and get it in writing that it was your idea!

To:
Fr:
Re:
Date:

I have been thinking about ways to help each salesperson manage their workload more efficiently, and I would like to make a suggestion for consideration.

Currently, there are no tools in place that allow salespeople uninterrupted time to concentrate on price quotes, correspondence, etc. I'd like you to consider putting a schedule in place so that each representative has a specified time to take incoming calls, make outbound calls, and be responsible for leads.

In order to make this program work, we would need to assure that all departments understood and complied with the call schedule. I have created a sample schedule to illustrate my thoughts, which I have attached. I would like to try this beginning next month, with my team. Please let me know your thoughts, and if I can count on your support for this new schedule.

Memo to Sales Manager: Eliciting Support for an Idea 2

To:

Fr:

Re:

Date:

I was reviewing some of the old sales programs that were utilized in past years, and I would like to bring back the "buy one/get one" program for [product]. The returns on that program were double any other program that year, and by spotlighting our new product, [Name], I think the chances are better than ever that we could see a significant return on our product offering.

Please let me know how you feel about taking this program "out of mothballs."

Keep ideas out there.

Memo to Other Departments: Eliciting Support for an Idea 1

To:

Fr:

Re:

Date:

The Inside Sales Team would like to try to change the way that we take inbound calls and leads.

Currently there is no set schedule in place to give sales representatives the opportunity to schedule their time, because each representative makes and receives calls throughout the day.

I would like to put a plan into affect that gives each sales rep a schedule so they know when to plan to receive any incoming calls and leads. This will require that the other departments that answer the general sales line be aware of what the schedule is and can abide by it.

It will require that your staff become more proactive about suggesting voice mail or sending the call to an alternate representative. The advantage for your staff is they know who will receive incoming calls at a given time each day, which will make trying to find an available sales representative less stressful for them.

Please discuss this with your team, and let me know your thoughts.

Soliciting feedback from other staff members is great internal relations and helps everyone think as a team.

Memo to Other Departments: Eliciting Support for an Idea 2

To:

Fr:

Re:

Date:

I read an article in the [Name] magazine and there is an opportunity to recommend our employer as "The best place to work" in the state.

I think that this is an opportunity for us to recognize [Employer] and thank them for all they do to make this an employee-nurturing environment. I'd like to know what your thoughts are on this opportunity and how we could present it to the employees.

Use memos to run ideas by other departments.

To Other Departments: Seeking Information about a Product 1

Keeping everyone abreast of the competition is important to be competitive.

To:

Fr:

Re:

Date:

Our Sales Team has been hearing about a new product called [Name], which appears to be in direct competition with our product, [Name]. I haven't been able to find out much about it, yet, but I believe it is manufactured by [Company], and has been on the market for about 6 months.

I'd like to know if any other departments have heard of this product, as it's possible customers are mentioning it to you. If you are hearing about it, or you can give me any information on how it works, please give me a call.

To Other Departments: Seeking Information about a Product 2

To:
Fr:
Re:
Date:

As you know, I requested any information on [Product] earlier this month. I have had several calls from other departments and have compiled some general information on this component.

I'd like to ask the Marketing Department to look into this in more detail, and to provide us with a cost and competitive analysis so that we can help our salespeople with the cross-sell. Let me know if you have any questions.

Investigate things that can help salespeople sell and run the ideas by the people who would need to use them.

Memo to Other Departments: Information on a Process 1

To:
Fr:
Re:
Date:

Use employees to voluntarily help investigate an idea.

We are considering upgrading our order processing systems and if we do so, will likely integrate it with some of the other processes currently being used. In order to create an order process that will meet everyone's needs, we would like to get your input on how you currently use order entry.

There is a brief questionnaire attached, which asks some basic questions about your interaction with the order process. Please fill out and return to me by the end of the week.

If you are interested in participating in a user group to help develop the new process please let me know.

Memo to Other Departments: Information on a Process 2

To:

Fr:

Re:

Date:

I am developing a new system to track the type of customer inquiries we receive, while the new database is under development. If you are currently use Excel or some other program to track information for your department, I'd appreciate it if you could give me a call, so I can develop a short-term solution similar to what other departments are using.

Always send out memos telling employees about ideas that are percolating for changes in the way they do things.

Memo to Other Departments: Resolving a Problem 1

Things like parking may seem unimportant, but disgruntled employees don't do as well at their work as they could if they are too busy grumbling over things like parking.

To:
Fr:
Re:
Date:

I'd like to get together with you and the other managers to see if we can come up with a solution to the parking issue. I know that the lack of available parking is something that we are all dealing with, and having our employees run out of the building several times a day to "feed the meter" is not a viable solution either.

I'm hoping if we all put our heads together we can brainstorm and hopefully present options to management. Let me know if you are available Friday at 10:00 and interested in participating.

Memo to Other Departments: Resolving a Problem 2

To:

Fr:

Re:

Date:

I'd like to put an item on the agenda for our Management meeting next week. We are experiencing an ongoing problem with calls being transferred to the wrong extensions, and I'm hoping we can talk about it and come up with some process to correct it.

I'm sure I don't need to tell you that our customers should not have to be transferred to more than one person to get the answers they need. Please put your thinking caps on, and plan to discuss at the meeting.

Don't let issues get to the boiling point. Mention them to management and offer suggestions as to how they can be resolved.

Memo to Other Departments: Thanking a Fellow Employee

There are lots of reasons to send memos to complain or mention things going wrong. Thank-you memos will be remembered.

To:
Fr:
Re:
Date:

I want to thank you for all you and your team has done to make my transition to management a little easier. This first week has been a challenge but thanks to your kindness and support it was also very productive.

Your kindness is appreciated.

Memo to Other Departments Giving Thanks

To:
Fr:
Re:
Date:

I want to thank you for letting us "borrow" [Name] to help us with our recent fax blast. [Name] showed great enthusiasm, was quick to learn, and was a big help in getting everything done and keeping it all collated so we can track the results.

I'm sure [Name] is a representative of all the great employees on your team, thanks again!

Always thank staff for accommodating changes and emergency needs.

Chapter 14

Letters for Promotion to Support Sales

Your sales force can do the best job they can selling when they come face-to-face with customers. In order to get prospects and retain customers, however, they need the support of the parent company to drive need and desire for products and services.

Promotion Letter

You can drive sales by creating promotions that let prospective buyers know they can't exist without your product or service. The general rule of thumb is that a person needs to see something three times before it sticks in their mind. So a well-placed ad in a trade magazine, followed by a publicity piece in a newsletter, followed up by a letter to a rented mailing list of the trade magazine's subscriber base—and the next time your sales staff calls on those customers, chances are they will be interested in hearing the pitch.

Press Releases

Releases of information to the news media, known as a press releases, can serve many purposes. A press release might announce a new product you now distribute or manufacture, a new employee you have hired, new partnerships you have entered into, or the move to your brand-new facility. Sometimes press releases are printed as you have written them, sometimes they are edited, sometimes they are the impetus for someone from a newspaper or magazine to do a bigger story on your company or your new product or the industry you are in.

Whatever specific purpose the press release serves, one of the main things it does is gain your company publicity. Every time your company name is in print, it is a chance to have it stick in the minds of someone who might be interested in buying your products or using your services.

In bigger companies, press releases will be written by the media or communications department. If your company does not have such a department, the sales manager should make sure to schedule regular press releases.

Letters to the Editor

A letter to the editor of your newspaper can serve to clarify an inaccurate depiction of or statement about your company made in a story in the paper. It may also serve as a public forum to thank an individual or group of people for something. Don't use it to gripe about things that you think are unfair. That just leaves a bad impression on people who read it and will work against you.

Press Release: New Product or Service 1

Press releases can be used to announce the status of new products in development. Even though the product may not be ready for immediate release, you'll want to start generating "buzz" before the product goes on sale.

FROM: [Company]

CONTACT: [Person distributing press release]

DATE: [Date]

FOR: Immediate Release

[Company] announced today that it has finished beta-testing on their new software product, "How to Write a Business Letter," and it will be released to the general public on [date].

This CD-Rom combines the complete text of the book as well as 700 letters in a searchable database format. This product is the companion to the previously released CD-Rom product "How NOT to Write a Business Letter."

#

Press Release: New Product or Service 2

FROM: [Company]

CONTACT: [Person distributing press release]

DATE: [Date]

FOR: Immediate Release

The Business Doctor, a local consulting firm specializing in upgrading technology for small businesses, announced today that it will offer a seminar, titled "Put a Smile in Your Voice and Lean Towards That Phone," designed for customer service, sales development, and inside sales staff.

Business Doctor president [Name] remarked that "while people answering the phone have enthusiasm, knowledge, and a desire to make every call count, there are common mistakes made every day that leave the caller with a less-than-desirable view of the company, by making simple conversational mistakes."

The seminar will be held on [date] at [Location]. Per person cost is [amount]. The Business Doctor is located at [Address] and can be found on the Internet at [[www.ww.com].

#

Send announcements of seminars, conferences, and trade shows to the business editor of the papers within the region of the event. Editors will use them to get the events into their calendar listings.

Press Release: New Hires 1

Always try to include a brief statement of general information about the company in a press release, probably toward the end after the key information. You can announce you hired a new rep for the Southeast territory, but if the reader doesn't know what your business does, it won't mean much to them.

FROM: [Company]

CONTACT: [Person distributing press release]

DATE: [Date]

FOR: Immediate Release

[Company] announced today that they have hired four new inside salespeople to accommodate the company's expansion.

[Name] will be responsible for inside sales in the Northeast region. Previously associated with a company located on the West Coast, [Name] has over 10 years experience in sales and marketing.

[Name] has joined [Company] after several years working in the banking industry, and will be responsible for inside sales in the Southeast.

For the Northeast territory, [Name] will join the company in October, after relocating from the Midwest, where she was an outside sales representative for the plumbing industry.

[Name], also originally from the Midwest, will handle inside sales for that territory. He recently completed his military service, including a tour of duty in Iraq.

[Company], a manufacturer of hardware and software used in call centers, is located in [City].

#

Press Release: New Hires 2

FROM: [Company]

CONTACT: [Person distributing press release]

DATE: [Date]

FOR: Immediate Release

[Company], an automotive sales and service organization located in [City], announced today that they have hired a new Service Manager. [Name], a factory trained and certified mechanic, will join [Company] on [date].

[Company] provides full service for the following vehicle types: [list] and is located at [address].

#

A new hire and his or her credentials is great publicity for a company.

Press Release: New Partnership 1

Partnerships, whether formal or informal, are great opportunities for press releases and publicity.

FROM: [Company]

CONTACT: [Person distributing press release]

DATE: [Date]

FOR: Immediate Release

The [Name] Company, manufacturer and marketer of fine chocolates, has announced a strategic partnership with [Name] winery. Their joint sales programs will provide consumers with the ability to purchase both products through catalog sales and web shopping-cart programs.

Details of a combined marketing and advertising program will be announced at a press conference next month.

#

Press Release: New Partnership 2

FROM: [Company]

CONTACT: [Person distributing press release]

DATE: [Date]

FOR: Immediate Release

[Name] and [Name], independent accounting consultants, have announced they intend to create a partnership, which will be known as [Company]. Their company will offer complete accounting and tax preparation services to the community, as well as on-site per-hour service, or by contract accounting services to local businesses.

They intend to open a new office in [Location] in the fall.

#

This more formal partnership, which is creating a third company, definitely deserves a press release and will probably result in publicity for the new company in the form of a feature in a local newspaper.

Damage Control Letter 1

[Date]

[Name]
[Company]
[Address]
[City, State, Zip]

Dear:

We are sending this letter to all our customers who purchased the [Product name]. We have received several phone calls regarding the electrical safety of our product, after the television program [Name] aired last week.

While we understand the concern programs like this generate, and we applaud [Network] for bringing this issue to the attention of the public, we'd like to point out that the product profiled in this report and our product, [Name], have no relation to one another.

Our product is UL listed, and is completely safe for use. Please take a moment and review the attached brochure, which outlines the testing and safety procedures involved in the manufacture of our product.

We hope this information alleviates any concerns you may have.

Sincerely,

[Name]
[Title]

False publicity, no matter how innocent, needs to be headed off at the pass as soon as possible.

Damage Control Letter 2

[Date]

[Name]
[Company]
[Address]
[City, State, Zip]

Dear:

We'd like to apologize to you and to all our valued customers for the recent shipping errors that caused many orders to be mis-shipped or lost in transit. We have been using new shipping software, which was dropping the zero from all zip codes. As a result, packages have been delayed and have had to be rescheduled for delivery in many instances.

No customer will incur additional freight charges as a result of this problem. We have made the adjustments to our software and things will be shipped correctly going forward.

We apologize for any inconvenience this may have caused. We appreciate your business.

Sincerely,

[Name]
[Title]

Always send an apology direct from the company to the consumer for general errors that result in inconvenience to the customer. It can be a significant expense of both time and money, but retaining customers is always a worthwhile pursuit.

Letter to the Editor: Acknowledging the Public 1

Tragedy can be a solidifying experience for a business and a community. A letter to the editor of the local paper is a great way to let an entire community know that you appreciate their being there in a time of need.

[Date]

[Name]
[Company]
[Address]
[City, State, Zip]

Dear:

The public support of our organization has been nothing short of amazing, and we would like to use this forum to express our gratitude to the many people who have helped us, as we recover from the fire that damaged our offices last week.

Beginning with the Fire Department, who responded so quickly, and with the Police Department, who kept traffic flowing smoothly and kept our property safe as we tried to salvage things from the building, our sincere thanks.

The Red Cross and Salvation Army were on hand to dispense food and drink to the rescue workers and as always their efforts are appreciated, and their dedication heartwarming.

There are so many other people to thank, and we are sure that for everyone we name, we will leave out someone who also deserves our appreciation. Please know that even if we don't name you specifically, our gratitude is just as sincere.

The countless businesses who have offered to make space in their buildings, who have offered the use of furniture and equipment, data storage, use of their on-site gym, and much more, are too many to list here. This community should be very proud of the companies that are in our community; their employees, who are your neighbors and friends, are a credit to all.

We'd like to mention special appreciation to the kids at the local elementary school, [Name], for taking the time to send us a handmade card. It meant more than words can express.

We'll be back in business as soon as we can and we'll rebuild in this wonderful community that we call home.

Sincerely,

[Name]
[Title]

Letter to the Editor: Acknowledging the Public 2

[Date]

[Name]
[Company]
[Address]
[City, State, Zip]

Dear:

We would like to thank everyone who attended our recent open house, as we celebrated the grand reopening of our business.

We continue to be grateful for all the support we received in these past months and we are committed to expanding our business and creating more jobs in this community.

We would also like to thank this newspaper for its accurate and thoughtful coverage of our story.

Sincerely,

[Name]
[Title]

All too often we only send a letter to the editor to correct mistakes in a story. Taking the time to thank a paper for a well-covered story can go a long way in both media and public relations.

Damage Control: Reacting to a News Story 1

This letter might ultimately result in the paper running a correction—which you might want to ask for outright in your letter. If the errors are egregious enough that lawsuits may evolve, the paper may actually run a whole new story.

[Date]

[Name]
[Company]
[Address]
[City, State, Zip]

Dear:

Our organization has experienced a reduction in workforce, due to loss of a government contract. There have been some stories written in this newspaper that have not stated the facts in their entirety, and on behalf of the management of [Company], I would like to set the record straight.

The phrase "layoffs were done randomly, and with no warning" is completely inaccurate. We held meetings with our employees as early as two months ago, and announced that it was possible that we would be reducing our workforce. At that time, employees who were scheduled for retirement in this calendar year were given the option to retire early, with no loss of benefits. The reduction in workforce was done according to seniority. Neither of these actions represent "random" acts.

Your reporter stated that he was present at the meeting held with all employees last month. We were not aware that a member of the press was present at a company meeting, since it was inside our facility, which requires an ID to enter. We question the veracity of this statement.

We did not change the employment status of our personnel with no thought, but with serious consideration and a lot of anguish. It is our hope to recall the majority of these employees before the end of the year. It would be helpful to our continued recovery if stories concerning the changes in our organization were reported with greater attention to accuracy.

Sincerely,

[Name]
[Title]

Damage Control: Reacting to a News Story 2

[Date]

[Name]

[Company]

[Address]

[City, State, Zip]

Dear:

Our organization has lost its leader, when our President [Name] passed away after a long illness. We at [Company] are grieving for the loss of our friend and mentor, and it will be a loss felt for months.

The feature story that you did on the history of our company and the biography of [Name] was thoughtful, sensitive, and a true depiction of the kindness and generosity of this man. We appreciate the way in which your reporter captured the spirit of our company, and our leader.

Sincerely,

[Name]

[Title]

Losing a president of a company, either through death, retirement, sudden illness, or voluntary termination, can generate negative publicity for the company. In the case of death, it should be acknowledged immediately. Retirement, termination, or other non-sudden departure of a key employee can make customers nervous about the viability of the company unless you preempt those concerns with public notices.

Letter to Trade Magazine 1

[Date]

[Name]
[Company]
[Address]
[City, State, Zip]

Dear:

Thank you for the informative and positive review you ran on our product, [Name], in the [Month] edition of [Magazine]. We appreciate all of the feedback the article generated, and as a result of several suggestions for a small design change on the ignition switch, which was mentioned by your reviewer, this change will be made in the next production run of this equipment.

We appreciate that a magazine of your caliber has made our company known to your readers.

Sincerely,

[Name]
[Title]

There is no need to respond to every review run on your products, unless there is a change made or planned as a result of a review.

Letter to Trade Magazine 2

[Date]

[Name]
[Company]
[Address]
[City, State, Zip]

Dear:

After months of engineering and beta testing, and months of speculation as to what "this" is, [Company] is pleased to announce that we will unveil our new product on October 3, 2006, at 1:00 p.m.

You are invited to attend a press-only screening of "this," and our team of R & D engineers will be on hand to answer your questions.

This will be your chance to see "this" before everyone else does. Please join us.

Sincerely,

[Name]
[Title]

Mystery is a great way to get attention, but you can't use it too often or its impact is lost.

Letter of Congratulations 1

Taking notice of the milestones of employees of other companies with whom you do business shows a great attention to detail and a caring that extends outside your own firm.

[Date]

[Name]
[Company]
[Address]
[City, State, Zip]

Dear:

Congratulations on your 10th anniversary as an employee of [Company]. Your efforts and contributions have not gone unnoticed, and we look forward to your continued years of service to our organization.

Sincerely,

[Name]
[Title]

Letter of Congratulations 2

[Date]

[Name]
[Company]
[Address]
[City, State, Zip]

Dear:

We'd like to congratulate all the employees, staff, and management of [Company] on the opening of their new facility. We welcome you to our community, and are sure you will find, as we have, great employees, and a great place to live.

Sincerely,

[Name]
[Title]

Business-to-business relationships, such as with the companies in your neighborhood, are important to establish and maintain.

Letter of Congratulations 3

Congratulate your employees on good overall performance. If your announcements and notices always focus on the bad things, morale will sink and employees will lose their enthusiasm for their work.

[Date]

[Name]
[Company]
[Address]
(City, State, Zip)

Dear:

We have had our best quarter in the history of the company, and all of our employees are to be commended for the hard work and perseverance that has made this possible. We appreciate everything you do, and the outstanding sales and low rate of return for complaints will kick off the second half of our year in grand fashion.

Keep up the good work.

Sincerely,

[Name]
[Title]

Letter of Congratulations 4

[Date]

[Name]
[Company]
[Address]
[City, State, Zip]

Dear:

Thanks for your quick response to our customer's unscheduled visit on Friday. The tour you put together of the manufacturing and shipping operations was exactly what the client needed to see. Your knowledge of all our operations was evident by the confident way you answered all his questions.

You are to be commended for being able to roll with the punches, and I want you to know that the way you handled [Customer name] is directly responsible for the repeat order he gave us today.

Thanks for being a great team player.

Sincerely,

[Name]
[Title]

Acknowledge an employee's contribution with specifics—in this case the employee's actions resulted in an order.

Invitation 1

[Date]

[Name]
[Company]
[Address]
[City, State, Zip]

Dear:

[Company] is planning an open house on [date] to celebrate the opening of our new facility and to kick off our fall sales campaign. As one of our valued customers, we'd like to invite you to this special event.

The open house will include a tour of our new facilities and a sneak peak at the products we will be offering beginning October 2006. Please let us know if you can attend this function as our guest.

Sincerely,

[Name]
[Title]

Don't let customers find out about special events by accident (or worse, not at all). Send a letter of invitation.

Invitation 2

[Date]

[Name]
[Company]
[Address]
[City, State, Zip]

Dear:

Our annual sales meeting will take place the week of [dates]. This is our yearly meeting for all sales, marketing, and customer service personnel. In addition to our kickoff and new product launch, we have a dinner at the beginning and end of the week, with guest speakers.

The purpose of this letter is to inquire if you would be available to speak at the kick-off dinner on Sunday [Date]. The theme of this year's sales meeting is "service" and we feel that someone with your background would be the ideal speaker to initiate the theme.

Please contact me if you are interested so that we can work out the details. I look forward to your favorable response.

Sincerely,

[Name]
[Title]

Good speakers at sales meetings can make or break the meeting's effectiveness and how long employees remember what was said. Good speakers are always busy, so invite potential speakers by letter well ahead of time to make sure to get into their calendar.

Letter of Apology 1

[Date]

[Name]
[Company]
[Address]
[City, State, Zip]

Dear:

Your letter outlining your dissatisfaction with our product has been forwarded to me. First, let me apologize for the inconvenience that receiving damaged freight has caused. I understand that these glass jars were to be used for gifts at your yearly sales meeting, and I can understand your frustration at being short 6 units.

While a certain amount of breakage is often unavoidable in cross-country shipments, it's always unfortunate when it occurs. We have replaced the 6 units, and are shipping them by next-day air at our expense. Please dispose of the damaged units as you wish. We will file a claim with the freight company using the photographs you supplied.

Again, please accept our apologies.

Sincerely,

[Name]
[Title]

Bad things happen. Plan to have to send a few apology letters in your sales career. As long as you take care of things in a timely and satisfactory manner, customers usually quickly forget.

Letter of Apology 2

[Date]

[Name]
[Company]
[Address]
[City, State, Zip]

Dear:

Thank you for your telephone call. I appreciate the distress our construction vehicles have caused you, and I apologize for any upset this has caused your household.

As a mother myself, I can well remember what it is like to try to get a newborn into a sleep pattern, and I can appreciate your frustration with the trucks driving by your home. We have made every effort to keep the disruption to a minimum, with trucks only moving between 8:00 a.m. and 3:00 a.m. This phase of the construction will be completed next week, so the noise will diminish considerably.

Please accept my congratulations on the birth of your child, and my apologies for the unavoidable noise from our construction vehicles.

Sincerely,

[Name]
[Title]

Acknowledging an inconvenience can go a long way to defusing a complaint. If the inconvenience is going to end soon, be sure to include that in the letter. You might even try including a gift certificate to, in this case, a local children's store to help appease the person who complained.

Sympathy Letter 1

People often avoid sympathy letters because they don't know what to say. Keep it simple and just let people know you are thinking of them in their time of sorrow.

[Date]

[Name]
[Company]
[Address]
[City, State, Zip]

Dear:

On behalf of your co-workers and friends here at [Company] I'd like to express our sympathy for your recent loss.

While words cannot take away the sorrow you are experiencing, please know that you are not alone at this time. We hope that your fond memories of [Deceased] will be a comfort to you at this time.

Sincerely,

[Name]
[Title]

Sympathy Letter 2

[Date]
[Name]
[Company]
[Address]
[City, State, Zip]

Dear:

We have heard of your recent loss and on behalf of all employees of [Company] please accept our sincere condolences.

At times like these, competition between companies means nothing, and friendship and support mean everything. Please know that you have our support and that you are in our thoughts at this time.

If there is anything we can do, please don't hesitate to contact us.

Sincerely,

[Name]
[Title]

Even competitors can set aside their differences to be sympathetic at a time of loss.

Thank-You Letter 1

There are never too many opportunities to thank repeat customers.

[Date]

[Name]
[Company]
[Address]
[City, State, Zip]

Dear:

On behalf of everyone at [Company], please accept our thanks for your continued business. We appreciate the loyalty you have shown us through your repeat business, and are committed to shipping every order as you have ordered, on time, and without problems.

Please let us know if there is anything we can do to serve you better. Thank you again for the confidence you place in us, through your business.

Sincerely,

[Name]
[Title]

Thank-You Letter

[Date]

[Name]
[Company]
[Address]
[City, State, Zip]

Dear:

Thank you for your donation to the scholarship fund in memory of [Name]. The outpouring of support from the community has overwhelmed us. These donations have been placed in a scholarship fund for the children of [Name], so that they can attend college after they graduate.

Please accept our thanks for your kind donation.

Sincerely,

[Name]
[Title]

Donations should always be acknowledged with a thank-you letter.

Chapter 15

Letters to Third Parties

There are many people who serve as go-betweens between you and your customers. These include distributors, promotional partners, chambers of commerce, mailing list brokers, advertising agencies, and the media outlets where your ads appear.

Distributors

Keep in touch with your distributors. Give them the information they need to move your product. You need to let them know if something about your product changes, especially improvements you make. Let them know if terms are going to change so they can adjust accordingly. Keep them enthused about your product and if their sales are below expected performance, let them know that but also help them get their sales back on track.

Promotional Partners

If you are going to go into partnership with other businesses, you need to keep up a healthy correspondence with them. Communication is key in making a partnership work. Let them know what you are up to, toss around ideas for promotion, invite them to sales meetings. Keep in touch.

Chambers of Commerce

The chamber of commerce in the town in which you do business is waiting to help you. Commerce is their business and improving and developing the business climate in their town is what they aim to do. Contact them for business information and send them letters and press releases about what your business is up to. Offer to host a Chamber-sponsored event, advertise in their publications—make use of what they do.

Mailing List Brokers

In order to get the most out of mailing lists you rent, communicate with your list brokers. Help them understand your business and provide them with the information they need to put together the best collection of lists for the promotion you have planned.

Advertising Agencies

If you use an ad agency, make sure they know your business. Advertising is expensive; you need to communicate with ad agencies to get the most for your money.

Media Outlets

Send press releases and updated information about your company to any sources of advertising that you use. Be sure they know enough about your company to include you in special promotions and special ad pages they create.

Letter to a Distributor 1

[Date]

[Name]
[Company]
[Address]
[City, State, Zip]

Dear:

We have completed our testing of the new software for form design, and are ready to ship it to distributors. Our plan is to make it available to a select number of distributors before general marketing.

Your company has been selected as one of the distributors for the initial product launch, in part because of the importance of our strategic partnership, and also because your team has more technical expertise and will be able to answer customer questions.

Information about the product is attached. I would like to attend one of your monthly sales training classes to go over the product in more detail. Please let me know if this can be arranged.

Sincerely,

[Name]
[Title]

Use your distributors for helping with new product launches. Ask them to provide follow-up information and be sure their sales staff is well trained in the new product.

Letter to a Distributor 2

[Date]

[Name]
[Company]
[Address]
[City, State, Zip]

Dear:

It has been two years since our company reviewed distributor contracts, and as part of our diligence for our IPO, we are asking each of our distributors to review and sign an updated contract.

The terms of the contract have not changed since you initially contracted to sell our products through your channel; we merely want to have updated information from each of our partners.

If you have any questions, please contact our legal department.

Sincerely,

[Name]
[Title]

Keep contracts and other formal paperwork with distributors up to date.

Letter to a Distributor 3

[Date]

[Name]
[Company]
[Address]
[City, State, Zip]

Dear:

It has been brought to our attention that your sales of [Product] have been below our minimum sell price. As you know, pricing is based on market value and what comparable products are selling for in your region.

Distributors are given certain latitude in determining the sell price, based on what other products or services they may be bundling with ours. There is a minimum, however, that distributor sales should not go below.

Please review the terms of our contract, and contact us with any questions.

Sincerely,

[Name]
[Title]

Using distributors means keeping track of things like consistency in selling price. These kinds of inconsistencies can give your company a bad reputation in the marketplace.

Letter to a Distributor 4

[Date]

[Name]
[Company]
[Address]
[City, State, Zip]

Dear:

We'd like to welcome you as a strategic partner, and distributor of our products. We are pleased you have selected our company to partner with, and will do everything possible to make this a successful arrangement for you.

A distributor information package is included for your reference. It contains product information, distributor pricing (your cost) suggested list, and contacts within our organization for ordering sales collateral, checking on orders, etc.

If there is anything else you need to get you started, please let us know.

Sincerely,

[Name]
[Title]

Distributors are important sales outlets for many companies. Be sure to make them feel like a welcome part of your company and provide them with everything they need for the relationship to be a success.

Letter to a Promotions Partner 1

[Date]

[Name]
[Company]
[Address]
[City, State, Zip]

Dear:

Although the holiday season is some months away, it's time again to start planning our calendar and other holiday gift promotional activities.

We plan to do the same desk calendar we have in past years, with updated picture, and include international holidays as well, to include our partners in Europe and the Pacific Rim.

Please send me updated pricing for 5,000 calendars, as well as any information you have on holiday gifts for small-to-large customers.

Sincerely,

[Name]
[Title]

If you use promotional products, be sure to plan well in advance for your holiday gifts.

Letter to a Promotions Partner 2

[Date]

[Name]
[Company]
[Address]
[City, State, Zip]

Dear:

The fundraiser for the American Cancer Society was a great success and we achieved donations 20% above our projected goal.

The success of this program would not have been possible without your support. We appreciate everything you and your staff did to help promote this event, and we know that we could not have accomplished this alone.

Thanks again for your help with this.

Sincerely,

[Name]
[Title]

]It usually takes more than one company to have a successful event like a fundraiser for a major non-profit. Be sure to thank everyone involved and let them know just what a success the fundraiser was and that you couldn't have done it without them.

Letter to Chamber of Commerce 1

The chamber of commerce in the town in which you plan to do business can be very helpful in your startup efforts, especially if you plan to bring employment opportunities to the region.

[Date]

[Name]
[Company]
[Address]
[City, State, Zip]

Dear:

Our company is new to this community, and we are interested in learning about membership requirements for the Chamber of Commerce.

We have a total of 350 employees in the state, 275 based in [City]. Please send an information package and membership application to my attention.

Sincerely,

[Name]
[Title]

Letter to Chamber of Commerce 2

[Date]

[Name]
[Company]
[Address]
[City, State, Zip]

Dear:

We are interested in advertising in the Chamber of Commerce annual "business community" magazine. Please send us all information regarding rates and available placements.

If you have any questions please contact me.

Sincerely,

[Name]
[Title]

Business-to-business relationships can be some of the most valuable relationships in your business. Be sure to keep your name in front of other businesses as much as possible.

Letter to Chamber of Commerce 3

[Date]

[Name]
[Company]
[Address]
[City, State, Zip]

Dear:

Our company has completed the building of our new corporate offices, and we would like to combine our grand opening with hosting a Chamber "Business After Hours." Please contact me at your earliest convenience so that I can begin planning.

Thank you in advance for your assistance.

Sincerely,

[Name]
[Title]

Hosting a chamber of commerce event can be a great way to let the business community know about your company.

Letter to Chamber of Commerce 4

[Date]

[Name]
[Company]
[Address]
[City, State, Zip]

Dear:

Thank you for referring [Company] to us. One of the benefits of Chamber membership that we find most helpful is the business-to-business referral program. I am including some additional business cards for our company, as your office indicated that they are out.

Please let me know if I can be of additional service. Thank you again for referring your members to us.

Sincerely,

[Name]
[Title]

Let your chamber of commerce know that you appreciate their efforts and which services they provide that are especially useful to you.

Letter to a Mail List Broker 1

[Date]

[Name]
[Company]
[Address]
[City, State, Zip]

Dear:

Your name has been given to me as a possible source for business-to-business mail lists. I am interested in mailing lists, by state, with the IT decision maker, for the following SIC Codes:

[list]

Please contact me with information regarding pricing, availability, and sorting parameters.

Sincerely,

[Name]
[Title]

Explore new leads for mailing list rental. Be sure the broker knows exactly what you are looking for; it is too expensive to rent lists and send mailings to get the wrong group of names.

Letter to a Mail List Broker 2

[Date]

[Name]
[Company]
[Address]
[City, State, Zip]

Dear:

I am writing to request credit for the attached list of prospects that we mailed, and had mail returned as undeliverable. Please check your list, and provide me with credit, including postage for these contacts that could not be used.

Thank you in advance for your cooperation.

Sincerely,

[Name]
[Title]

Don't hesitate to ask for credit for returned mail from lists you bought from brokers. Not only do you want to use your resources wisely, but the list broker will want to know what names to purge from their lists.

Letter to a Mail List Broker 3

[Date]

[Name]
[Company]
[Address]
[City, State, Zip]

Dear:

I am writing to inquire about the range of services you offer. I am interested in learning if your mail list capabilities include sorting and scrubbing of lists that I currently own. If this is not a service you provide, I would appreciate any referral you would care to provide.

Sincerely,

[Name]
[Title]

Keep your own mailing lists as up-to-date as possible. If this is not something you can do yourself, find someone who can help. Let them know exactly what service you are looking for.

Letter to a Mail List Broker 4

[Date]

[Name]
[Company]
[Address]
[City, State, Zip]

Dear:

We have used your services in the past with great success and are planning on doing another mailing in the fall. We would like to do a 2-part mailing, so I am inquiring if we can purchase our list with a 2-run option. Please let me know if this is possible, and what charges that would incur.

Sincerely

[Name]
[Title]

Mail list brokers usually keep pretty good records of your uses of their lists. They should be able to readily identify what you used in the past if you want to use it again.

Letter to Ad Agency 1

Ad agencies can be very helpful and cost-effective as long as you take the time to find the right one for your business.

[Date]

[Name]
[Company]
[Address]
[City, State, Zip]

Dear:

Your agency has been recommended to me as one who specializes in promoting companies with a diverse product mix. I am interested in speaking with a representative to discuss our print and media needs for the coming year.

Please have an agency representative contact me at your earliest convenience.

Sincerely,

[Name]
[Title]

Letter to Ad Agency 2

[Date]

[Name]
[Company]
[Address]
[City, State, Zip]

Dear:

We'd like to congratulate you on the campaign you put together for [Company]. We found the television commercials to be particularly well thought out. As we are interested in contracting a new agency for our advertising, we'd like to talk with you.

If you are accepting new clients, and want to discuss our goals in more detail we would like to meet with you next week. Please give me a call to set up an appointment.

Sincerely,

[Name]
[Title]

If you like what you see from an ad agency, try to use them.

Letter to Ad Agency 3

[Date]

[Name]
[Company]
[Address]
[City, State, Zip]

Dear:

This letter is to inform you that we are exercising our 30-day clause to cancel our contract with you for print representation. As you know, we have brought to your attention on a number of occasions our concern about the lack of follow-up on the part of our representative, who rarely returns calls and has cancelled appointments with us at the last minute.

Since we are unable to obtain a resolution, we must seek representation from an agency more attuned to our needs. We regret this is necessary, but we thank you for the work that your agency has done on our behalf.

Sincerely,

[Name]
[Title]

If things aren't working out, look into your legal right to cancel your contract, cut your losses, and run.

Letter to Ad Agency 4

[Name]
[Company]
[Address]
[City, State, Zip]

Dear:

Recently we had an urgent issue come up and I wanted to write and let you know how much I appreciate the quick response from your agency representative.

The local television station contacted us by voice mail and wanted to include our company in an interview about businesses expanding in the valley. As luck would have it, I was out of town, as was [Name], who normally handles our media needs through your agency.

Although unfamiliar with our account, [Name] was able to contact both our representative and myself, get the information to us, and even offered to "pinch hit" with the interview.

This kind of service is why your agency is so successful, and why we chose you. Please accept our thanks.

Sincerely,

[Name]
[Title]

Don't hesitate to give thanks where it is due and compliment someone on a job you appreciated.

Letter to Media 1

Sending letters regarding rate cards gets you information for your files and gives the media outlet something concrete to start a file for you on their end. The sooner they get to know your business, the better service they can provide.

[Date]

[Name]
[Company]
[Address]
[City, State, Zip]

Dear:

We are interested in using your magazine as the key advertising media for our print needs. We would ideally like to run 4-color, quarter-page advertisements each month. Please provide me with your current rate card and placement guarantees.

Thank you in advance.

Sincerely,

[Name]
[Title]

Letter to Media 2

[Date]

[Name]
[Company]
[Address]
[City, State, Zip]

Dear:

We are planning a multi-media advertising campaign for the spring of 2007, to coincide with the marketing of a new line of products for recreational use.

Please send us all available information, including rate cards for print, radio, television, and direct mail advertising available through your publishing organization.

Thank you for your attention to our request.

Sincerely,

[Name]
[Title]

Multi-media campaigns are complex. Explore potential outlets and solicit their help as soon as possible.

Chapter 16

International Sales Letters

Business transactions with companies in other parts of the world are a common practice today. Our ability to access information and communicate it to a global audience has evolved with the evolution of technology.

But our ability to communicate information, while global, requires that consideration be given to two key factors: what message is being communicated, and who will be on the receiving end of the message.

You Say Potato—I Say Potahto

Imagine that you are an English-speaking customer in another part of the world and you have contacted a business in the U.S. to place an order. The person in the U.S. tries to reassure his client that this kind of request is common, using the phrase "all in a day's work." But this American businessperson has just implied that whatever the international client wants, it will be available in a single work day. Yikes! Problems dealing with international customers or vendors frequently are the result of poor communication, even when, as in this case, the two parties are speaking the same language.

Literal translation from one language to another can also cause problems. A common illustration of this point is that of General Motors and their Latin American advertising campaign for the Chevrolet Nova. If only one person had realized that the literal translation of "No Va" to Spanish is "No Go," General Motors might have named this automobile something different—at least for its Spanish-speaking customers!

> Noting that someone has made an error is hard to do in any language! While it's important to say that you feel an error has been made, the niceties of international business suggest that whenever possible you should not place any blame, just make a generic inquiry so that the person on the other end can save face.

Idioms

The dictionary defines the word "idiom" as: "A style or manner of expression peculiar to a given people." When do you use an idiom when composing an international sales letter? Never! Translation is often literal, and can create a situation ranging from confusion to insult. Here are just a few of our favorite expressions that can be found in sales letters, which when translated literally don't mean the same thing the world over:

- By the way
- Bare bones
- Cutthroat
- Flooding the market
- Explore every avenue
- Lame excuse
- Pet name
- Priced out of the market
- Sharp tongued
- Splitting hairs

Read your letters carefully to pick out these and other idioms and clichés and rephrase them with very general language, such as changing "we will explore every avenue" to "we will look into every possible way of doing this job."

The Value of Simplicity

Americans tend to be less formal in their communication with one another and have become sloppy in their letter writing. When composing a letter to someone in another country, however, it's often helpful to go back to the "old rules" for things like punctuation.

When communicating to a global audience, the best way to get your point across, and earn the appreciation of your recipient, is to present the information in a format that is easy to read and understand. The preceding sentence, for example, may have too many commas for the American audience but is a good example of breaking a sentence down for non-native English speakers/readers so that the message is given in blocks. Short declarative statements are easier to translate and keep the reader focused on the message, rather than the vocabulary. Inserting commas and semicolons will help the reader understand when to pause.

Some Formatting Details

International letters tend to use the Full-Block, or Block format. This means:

- In "full-block format" all the elements of the letter begin flush left.

- In "block format" the date, reference line, closing, and signature block are to the right of the center of the page
- "Modified block" is not often used in international correspondence. It is similar to the block format except paragraphs are indented.

If you or your company compose international correspondence frequently, it's better to standardize your letter type. Not only can you create a template, but also having all of your correspondence look the same will help to minimize confusion.

Dates should always be spelled out to avoid confusion. For example, write May 3, 2005, not 5/3/2005. Using 5/3/2005 means May 3 to you and me, but to many other people, including the English-speaking United Kingdom, it would mean the 5th of March. And it is better to be specific about time-frames than saying things like "in early spring"—don't forget, spring in at least half the world is opposite from your spring.

Salutation

Forms of address vary all over the world and we could devote an entire chapter to listing how to address letters, by country. A quick rule of thumb is to keep it formal, address your letter using either Mr. or Mrs./Miss (Ms. is not as common in letters coming from another county), or use a title if one has been given. When you have received a letter from someone who has addressed you formally, return the courtesy. When in doubt, ask!

In Asian cultures the last name is typically first. Therefore, a letter addressed to Mr. Toshihito Hata would begin with the salutation, Dear Mr. Toshihito. Japanese will often give you a hint by referring to one another as "san." Toshihito San is a respectful and less formal way to speak to Mr. Toshihito, but not in your initial letter! That type of address is better used once a relationship has developed, and then should be used carefully and in the right circumstances.

The way your letters close is also an important component and over-familiarity can create problems. "With warm regards," something we see frequently in letters in the U.S., is considered too personal in many parts of the world. "Sincerely" or "Regards" is often used when communicating with someone for the first time.

The Soft Sell

Good manners are an important part of all correspondence, and again there is a significant cultural difference between countries in how questions are asked, information is given, and conflicts are resolved. The tone of a letter is as important as the way it's worded and will have an impact in how quickly and how satisfactorily the business is handled. Americans would think nothing of sending a "demand for payment" letter worded: "Full payment of the past due invoice is expected within 10 days, or other action will be taken."

Writing a more carefully worded past due invoice to someone overseas would yield a better result: "We would appreciate your attention to this matter, and would like to hear from you concerning this misplaced invoice within 10 days, if possible."

Everyone knows the invoice isn't missing, it's just not paid, but asking for payment, rather than demanding it, allows the recipient to save face, and take care of the matter promptly.

English is considered to be the universal language of business, but we can't forget it's not the only language spoken in the world. Taking some time to understand the business practices, cultures, and niceties of doing business in another county will give you an advantage over those who compete for business as though they were in their own backyard.

Letter of Inquiry 1

[Date]

[Name]
[Company]
[Address]
[City, State, Zip]

Dear:

Here is the information you requested. The training manual will also provide you with guidelines for selling this product to your customers.

The processes required to obtain a license to import are fairly strict, and you should consult your solicitor or agent to assure that you can meet each requirement. Once you have ascertained that you are able to secure the licenses needed, we can discuss in more detail what you will need for an initial investment.

Please let me know if I can be of additional help.

Sincerely,

[Name]
[Title]

Don't offer any speculation on information about selling internationally that you are not completely sure of. Direct potential licensors to the places that can help them.

Letter of Inquiry 2

[Date]

[Name]
[Company]
[Address]
[City, State, Zip]

Dear:

In response to your letter asking for additional information, I am enclosing details on how the system operates. I would be happy to provide you with a quote based on the modules you feel would be best suited to your environment.

I hope that the enclosed information will help you evaluate how our [product] can exceed your expectations. I appreciate your interest and look forward to hearing from you.

Sincerely,

[Name]
[Title]

You will need to be willing to offer as much backup support as needed to sell internationally.

Cover Letter: Response to Request for Credit

[Date]

[Name]
[Company]
[Address]
[City, State, Zip]

Dear:

Congratulations! Your company's request for credit has been approved and a new account has been opened with a line of credit of [amount].

Please take a moment to familiarize yourself with our terms and conditions, as they apply to your account. If you have any questions or concerns, please let me know, and I will be happy to clarify the details.

The credit representative who will handle your account is [Name] and I am including [his/her] contact information for your convenience. I know that [Name] will be happy to help you.

We look forward to working with you.

Sincerely,

[Name]
[Title]

You should be willing to extend credit to overseas customers, but be sure to go through all the usual credit-check channels that you do with all customers. Collecting from delinquent international accounts can be a bit harder than local collecting.

Dunning Letter

[Date]

[Name]
[Company]
[Address]
[City, State, Zip]

Dear:

Thank you for your order of [date]. I noticed that your initial invoice is now more than 45 days past due. Since we discussed our payment terms in our initial correspondence, I'm sure this is an oversight, and have included a copy of your invoice for your convenience.

Thank you for your attention to this, and please let me know if I can be of assistance.

Sincerely,

[Name]
[Title]

Be courteous according to international standards but also be prompt in attempting to resolve unpaid invoices.

Inaccurate Payment Amount

Point out inaccuracies in international payments quickly. Indicate in the letter you assume it was a mistake but expect resolution.

[Date]

[Name]
[Company]
[Address]
[City, State, Zip]

Dear:

Thank you for your check in the amount of [amount]. The full amount has been applied to your invoice [number]. I am wondering if there was a typographical error when the check was printed, as the dollar and cent amount paid is reversed from the invoice. I am including a copy of the invoice, as well as a copy of your check, so that you can review it with your payables staff.

Please let me know if you need any additional information, as my associates and I are at your service.

Sincerely,

[Name]
[Title]

International Sales Letter 1

[Date]

[Name]
[Company]
[Address]
[City, State, Zip]

Dear:

I would like your assistance in selecting a site in your country for our business.

[Company] is interested in locating a site suitable for a distribution center, which will process and ship all orders going to our international customers. We are interested in an arrangement that would allow us to lease space. Details regarding the size, location preference, and number of anticipated employees are enclosed.

As we evaluate locations for this business, we must know if the following are available, and, if so, what are the costs associated with each of them:

- Transportation by ground and air methods
- Warehouse space
- Utilities and other associated overhead costs
- Housing and schools for employees and their families.

We would like to receive this information no later than [date] so that we can plan our visits accordingly. Thank you for your help.

Sincerely,

[Name]
[Title]

Send letters with details for help from people on the ground in the country in which you are interested in doing business.

International Sales Letter 2

[Date]

[Name]
[Company]
[Address]
[City, State, Zip]

Dear:

I would like to learn about becoming an importer of your [product]. My company, [Name], is the premier importer for [product] and we feel that expanding our line of products to include [Product name] will provide a wider range of [equipment/accessories] to our existing customers as well as attract new prospects.

Please provide me with information concerning your price scale, minimums, if required, terms and conditions, and any information on duties and taxes. As I have not done business with your country before, I would appreciate any recommendation you may have for brokers and Air Cargo Expeditors.

A brochure with information regarding our company and current product line is included. I look forward to hearing from you at your earliest convenience.

Sincerely,

[Name]
[Title]

International letter standards are the same whether you are looking to import or export.

International Sales Letter 3

[Date]

[Name]
[Company]
[Address]
[City, State, Zip]

Dear:

Thank you for your inquiry. We appreciate your visiting our web site [www.ww.com] and sending us your feedback.

We do not have a program for customers outside of the United States at this time. The nature of our product is specific to U.S. regulatory guidelines and has not been modified for an international market.

There is a possibility that we will develop a similar product, which will meet the standards of [Country] in the future, and we will gladly keep your inquiry on file for this possibility.

Sincerely,

[Name]
[Title]

Don't just say you will keep their information on file, do it. You never know when you are going to want to expand your business; having a list of potential international distributors on hand could prove valuable.

Letter of Introduction 1

Looking things over in person is the best way to do business in a foreign country. Set up meetings and tours well in advance to give international businesses with which you would like to do business plenty of time to prepare for your visit.

[Date]

[Name]
[Company]
[Address]
[City, State, Zip]

Dear:

Please accept this letter as our introduction to you. [Company] has been in business since [year], and [Name] and I will be visiting your country from [dates]. We would like to arrange a meeting with you for the purpose of visiting your manufacturing facility. The type of manufacturing process you are using is of particular interest to us, as we hope to use a similar process for our products.

Our agent, [Name], will contact you next week to confirm a more specific date and itinerary for our visit. We look forward to meeting you and learning more about your company, and look forward to your favorable response.

Sincerely,

[Name]
[Title]

Letter of Introduction 2

[Date]

[Name]
[Company]
[Address]
[City, State, Zip]

Dear:

This letter is to introduce my trusted associate, [Name], who will be visiting your country for the purpose of meeting our international suppliers. [Name] has been with our company since [date] and his duties include maintaining all contractual agreements with our suppliers. [Name] will be in [Country] during the week of [dates].

I am sure that you will find [Name] to be well versed in the manufacturing processes used in [product] and I am equally confident that he will enjoy the same courtesy you have extended to me, during my visits.

[Name] will contact you to make appointment arrangements. We value our relationship with [Company] and look forward to a continued partnership.

Sincerely,

[Name]
[Title]

In international business, introductions are very important.

Thank-You Letter 1

[Date]

[Name]
[Company]
[Address]
[City, State, Zip]

Dear:

Thank you for your interest in distributing [Product] in [Country]. The options for purchasing our product internationally have been somewhat limited, and my partners and I would like to explore this opportunity with you in more detail.

Each of the distributors currently working with our company are operating as independent channel partners, and have been able to offer our products at a competitive price, because the options for [Product] have been limited outside of the United States.

Your cost will vary depending on the range of products and quantities you select, but I have included a price list to give you an idea of the cost/sell ratio.

Once you have reviewed the pricing and contracts please call or e-mail me so that we can discuss them in detail. I look forward to speaking with you again, and working with you in the future.

Sincerely,

[Name]
[Title]

If a foreign company expresses interest in your product, use the opportunity to do some market research and explore the idea with an interested party.

Thank-You Letter 2

[Date]

[Name]
[Company]
[Address]
[City, State, Zip]

Dear:

Thank you for all the courtesies you extended me during my recent visit to your country. I was delighted with the sites you selected as possible manufacturing and warehousing locations, and will evaluate all the data you thoughtfully provided.

I hope that this visit was one of many to come, as we develop our relationship with your country, and its citizens.

Sincerely,

[Name]
[Title]

Always follow up a foreign visit with a thank-you letter. It takes time and staff resources to prepare for a visit and this simple courtesy will be appreciated.

Thank-You Letter 3

[Date]

[Name]
[Company]
[Address]
[City, State, Zip]

Dear:

Thank you for responding to my inquiry. I have reviewed the catalog and ordering information that you provided, and have researched the terms and conditions for importation of [Product] to my country.

I have forwarded the contracts to my solicitor and expect to meet with him early next week. I will be in touch with any questions or comments he might have. I expect that we will reply favorably to your offer, and look forward to speaking with you soon.

Sincerely,

[Name]
[Title]

Follow up the receipt of international materials with a thank-you letter explaining what you plan to do next.

Thank-You Letter 4

[Date]

[Name]
[Company]
[Address]
[City, State, Zip]

Dear:

Thank you for sending me the samples of your product for evaluation. I was pleased with the quality and workmanship and would like to consider including these items in our Winter/Holiday catalog. I am including a sales projection, and would appreciate a price quote based on the total projection in one order, as well as the total projection purchased in three equal shipments.

Once I have reviewed the pricing, I will be in touch with you within a week to finalize our agreement. I look forward to offering my customers the finely crafted products made by [Company].

Sincerely,

[Name]
[Title]

It cost companies real money to send samples to potential international clients. Be sure to thank them and tell them your plans.

Check Your Proofreading Ability!

Each of the letters on the following pages has the accurate version on the left side and the version with mistakes on the right. First, cover over the letter on the left and find any general typos and mistakes you can in the letter on the right. Then, uncover the letter on the left to see how good you are at comparing the two letters to find mistakes. Then to check your proofreading, look at the end to find each letter with the mistakes highlighted.

November 12, 2004

Jason Collier

Anderson Asphalt Company
2169 Jackson Avenue
Biloxi, MI 82364^MS?

Dear Mr. Collier,

This is to confirm our conversation of November 10 at the Radisson Hotel conference about scheduling the repaving of our company parking lot. Thanks for accommodating our desire to complete this job during the Christmas week shut-down of our factory. You also thought you could recommend a subcontractor to paint in the lines for parking spaces. I'd appreciate it if you would send me that contact information by return mail, Jason.

Here are the details I promised to send to you. Our parking lot is 200 x 350', for a total of 70,000 square feet. You quoted us a price of $5.50 per square foot, including the removal of existing pavement and preparing the surface for new asphalt. The price we agreed on is $385,000. You agreed that work would begin on December 26, 2004, estimated to be completed in four business days.

If you can confirm the above dates and costs on a contract to be received by us before November 23 and schedule your crews accordingly, we will send you the agreed upon 10% deposit of $38,500 by December 20, 2004. Jackson Ball Bearings looks forward to doing business with you.

Sincerely,

Stuart Jackson, Vice President
Jackson Ball Bearing Company
673 Collier Street
Biloxi, MI 82606

November 12, 2004

Jason Collier

Anderson Asphalt Company
2196 Jackson Avenue
Biloxi, MI 82364

Dear Ms. Collier,

This is to confirm our conversation of November 10 at the Radisson Hotel conference about scheduling the repaving of our company parking lot. Thanks for accommodating our desire to complete this job during the Christmas week shut-down of our factory. You also thought you could recommend a subcontractor to paint in the lines for parking spaces. I'd appreciate it if you would send me that contact information by return mail, John.

Here are the details I promised to send to you. Our parking lot is 200 x 350', for a total of 60,000 square feet. You quoted us a price of $5.50 per square foot, including the removal of existing pavement and preparing the surface for new asphalt. The price we agreed on is $358,000. You agreed that work would begin on December 26, 2004, estimated to be completed in four business days.

If you can confirm the above dates and costs on a contract to be received by us before November 23 and schedule your crews accordingly, we will send you the agreed upon 10% deposit of $58,500 by December 20, 2004. Jackson Ball Bearings looks forward to doing business with you.

Sincerely,

Stewart Jackson, Vice President
Jackson Ball Bearing Company
673 Collier Street
Biloxi, MI 86206

September 8, 2003

Beverly Crawford
Miami Humane Society
3749 Sunset Street
Miami, FL 47261

Dear Ms. Crawford,

Thanks for your phone call last week regarding the purchase of 185 doses of distemper vaccines and 310 units of heartworm medication. We are pleased to inform you that we can accommodate your order at the discount price discussed.

Please sign the attached contract and confirm quantities, prices, and requested shipping dates. Return it to us promptly to reserve your order. Because vaccinations must be refrigerated, please allow an extra three days for the carrier to schedule a shipment.

Our company will also send ten boxes of our new flea preventative with your order at no extra charge. It is our pleasure to support animal shelters in their important work. Thanks for the opportunity to serve you.

Sincerely,

Althea Day
Fido's Healthcare Company
2131 South Harvard Road
Stanhope, OH 57248

September 8, 2003

Beverly Crawford
Miami Humane Society
3947 Sunset Street
Miami, FL 47261

Dear Ms. Crawford,

Thanks for your phone call last week regarding the purchase of 185 doses of distemper vaccines and 210 units of heartworm medication. We are pleased to inform you that we can accommodate your order at the discount price discussed.

Please sign the attached contract and confirm quantities, prices, and requested shipping dates. Return it to us promly to reserve your order. Because vacinations must be refrigerated, please allow an extra three days for the carrier to schedule a shipment.

Our company will also send ten boxes of our new flea preventative with your order at no extra charge. It is our pleasure to support animal shelters in their important work. Thanks for the opportunity to serve you.

Sincerely,

Althea Day
Fido's Healthcare Company
2131 South Harvard Road
Stanhipe, OH 57248

April 23, 2003

Carol Dexter
Nova Services
28 Parkside Drive
Toledo, OH 59732

Dear Ms. Dexter,

I have noticed a discrepancy on the bill we received from your company dated April 19. The amount charged for Sandra Moriarty for two weeks of temporary receptionist services exceeds our contract by $75.

Sandra worked for a total of 60 hours. Our contract states that her hourly rate would be $7.25. However, we were billed at an hourly rate of $8.10, for a total of $510.00. The contracted total was $435.00.

Thanks for checking into this for us, Carol. Upon receipt of a corrected invoice, we will send payment.

Sincerely,

Suki Yoshuru
Accounts Payable
Good Hands Insurance
3438 Tower Way
Emmaus, PA 26743

April 23, 2003

Carol Dexter
Nova Services
29 Parkside Drive
Toledo, OH 59723

Dear Ms. Dexter,

I have noticed a discrepincy on the bill we received from your company dated April 19. The amount charged for Sandra Morirty for two weeks of temporary receptionist services exceeds our contract by $75.

Sandra worked for a total of 60 hours. Our contract states that her hourly rate would be $6.25. However, we were billed at an hourly rate of $8.10, for a total of $510.00. The contracted total was $453.00.

Thanks for checking into this for us, Carol. Upon receipt of a corrected invoice, we will send payment.

Sincerely,

Suki Yoshuri
Accounts Payable
Good Hands Insurance
3483 Tower Way
Emmaus, PA 27643

September 4, 2002

Jose Perez
Peterson's Flooring Emporium
583 Hudson Avenue
Peekskill, NY 12749

Dear Mr. Perez,

Your services were recommended by a friend, Sadie Lamb, who was a customer several years ago. We admired the tile your company provided and installed in her home. We have tried to match it in our local area, without success.

Sadie can't remember just when the work was done, nor does she have the receipt that might give details about ordering the tile. We hope that your records might provide the missing information. We provide Sadie's address and telephone number to help you find her in your files. She is happy to confirm her agreement to this process, if you want to contact her.

> Sadie Lamb
> 37 Elm Street
> La Grange, NY 12643
> (212) 555-3478

If you can identify the tile that went into Sadie's house and had it in stock or could order it, we would love to discuss the details of purchasing it from you. We hope you can help!

Truly yours,

Bob and Linda Grimes
389 Freedom Drive
Farmington, NY 12543

September 4, 2002

Jose Perez
Peterson's Flooring Emporium
583 Hudson Avenue
Peekskill, NY 12749

Dear Mr. Perez,

Your services were recommended by a friend, Sadie Lamb, who was a custemer several years ago. We admired the tile your company provided and installed in her home. We have tried to match it in our local area, without success.

Sadie can't remember just when the work was done, nor does she have the receipt that might give details about ordering the tile. We hope that your records might provide the missing inf^irmation. We provide Sadie's address and telephone number to help you find her in your files. She is happy to confirm her agreement to this process, if you want to contact her.

> Sadie Jenkins
> 73 Elm Street
> La Grange, NY 12643
> (212) 555-3874

If you can identify the tile that went into Sadie's house and had it in stock or could order it, we would love to discuss the det^ials of purchasing it from you. We hope you can help!

Truly yours,

Bob and Linda Jenkins
389 Freedom Drive
Farmington, NY 12543

March 11, 1999

Sarah Peavey

Sunny Acres Farm

91 Farm Ridge Road

Blaine, MT 64931

Dear Ms. Peavey,

As you may know, Saddle Up Stables in Blaine are for sale. I am considering buying the property as a boarding and lesson facility. In my long-distance discussions with the current owner, your name was mentioned as a possible source for quality hay.

I anticipate that I would require between 7,200 and 7,400 bales a year. The loft at Saddle Up will hold a month's worth, or about 600 bales. Would your fields provide that amount of hay annually? Would monthly delivery and unloading be possible to arrange?

If the answer is yes to these questions, I'd be happy to speak with you about establishing a relationship. I'll be out of the country until the end of April. Please contact me at the address below to let me know if you are interested. If not, do you know any other local hay producers who might be? Thanks in advance for your time.

Best,

Lonnigan Brady

92 Cambridge Street

Malden, MA 02568

March 11, 1999

Sarah Peevey

Sunny Acres Farm

91 Farm Ridge Road

Blaine, MI 64931

Dear Ms. Peavey,

As you may know, Saddle Up Stables in Blaine are for sale. I am considering buying the property as a b^aording and lesson facility. In my long-distance discussions with the current owner, your name was mentioned as a possible source for quality hay.

I anticipate that I would require between 7,200 and 8,400 bales a year. The loft at Saddle Up will hold a month's worth, or about 600 bales. Would your feilds provide that amount of hay annualy? Would monthly delivery and unloading be possible arrange?

If the answer is yes to these questions, I'd be happy to speak with you about establishing a relationship. I'll be out of the country until the end of April. Please contact me at the adress below to let me know if you are interested. If not, do you any other local hay producers who might be? Thanks in advance for your time.

Best,

Lonnigan Brody

92 Cambridge Street

Malden, MA 02865

May 2, 1998

Candid Camera Shoppe
Customer Service Department
89 Holly Corner
Granville, IL 34185

Greetings.

In 1989, I purchased a Nikon 35mm SLR camera from you, with a very special telephoto lens made in Denmark, for photographing tiny things. I specialize in Victorian miniatures. The camera took marvelous photographs for 10 years. Sadly, I dropped the lens and cracked it. I'm hoping it can be repaired.

I have inquired in my local area, but no one seems to have access to parts or service for this lens. I'm hoping that you do. It's a Bjorklund 9600, 400mm lens. I'm happy to ship it to you from California, where I now live, if your service team can help. Can you?

Sincerely,

Arthur Toggenburg
236748 Pacific Boulevard
Del Coronado, CA 92618
(673) 845-1989

May 2, 1998

Candid Camera Shop
Customer Srvice Department
89 Holly Corner
Granville, IL 34185

Greetings.

In 1989, I purchased a Nikon 335mm SLR camera from you, with a very special telephoto lens made in Denmark, for photographing tiny things. I specialize in Victorian minitures. The camera took marvelous photographs for 10 years. Sadly, I dropped the lens and cracked it. I'm hoping it can be repired.

I have inquired in my local area, but no one seems to have axxess to parts or service for this lens. I'm hoping that you do. It's a Biorklund 9700, 400mm lens. I'm happy to ship it to you from California, where I now live, if your service teem can help. Can you?

Sincerely,

Arthur Togginberg
236749 Pacific Buolevard
Del Coronado, CA 92618
(674) 845-1998

April 14, 2003

Fins and Shells Seafood Company
ATTN: Marcy Delrio
24 Ocean Blvd.
New Bedford, MA 02634

Dear Ms. Delrio,

We here at the Community Vocational College are excited about the graduation clambake your company has agreed to cater for us on June 7 this year. To confirm our conversation earlier this week, here are the details.

We are expecting 52 graduates and 104 guests, as well as 25 faculty and staff. To feed these 181 people, you advised that we would require:

250 pounds of clams,

250 stuffed quahogs,

200 ears of corn,

100 pounds of potato salad,

75 pounds of green salad,

25 pounds of Indian pudding,

and 50 pounds of vanilla ice cream.

Your company will also provide soft drinks, bottled water, coffee and tea for the gathering. Your staff will arrive at 10AM on June 7 to set up the food in time for the 2PM clambake. The bake pit will have been dug for your staff in advance. By 5PM that day, your staff will have completed the clean-up.

We will send a deposit of $2,354, half the contracted price, upon receipt of a written contract from Fins and Shells.

Thanks in advance for your excellent service and food.

Sincerely,

Barbara Jones
Events Coordinator
CVC
3472 Fairhaven Rd.
Fall River, MA 02573

April 14, 2003

Fins and Shells Seafood Company
ATTN: Marc Delrio
24 Ocean Blvd.
New Bedford, MA 02634

Dear Mr. Delrio,

We here at the Community Vocationl College are excited about the graduation lambake your company has agreed to cater for us on June 6 this year. To confirm our conversation earlier this week, here are the details.

We are expecting 52 graduates and 401 guests, as well as 25 faclty and staff. To feed these 131 people, you advised that we would require:

250 pounds of clams,

250 stuffed quahogs,

200 ears of corn,

100 pounds of potatoe salad,

25 pounds of green salad,

75 pounds of Indian pudding,

and 50 pounds of vanilla ice cream.

Your company will also provide soft drinks, bttled water, coffee and tea for the gathering. Your staff will arrive at 10AM on June 9 to set up the food in time for the 2AM clambake. The bake pit will have been dug for your staff in advance. By 5PM that day, your staff will have completed the clean-up.

We will send a deposit of $2,534, half the contracted price, upon receipt of a written contract from Fins and Smells.

Thanks in advance for your excellent service and food.

Sincerely,

Barbara Jones
Events Coordinater
CVC
3472 Fairhaven Rd.
Fall River, MA 02573

September 8, 2004

Basil Rathbone
Good Times Marina
459 Ocean Way
Camden, ME 04582

Dear Mr. Rathbone,

Thanks for your interest in our de-icing system. Free Docks offers a patented system that guarantees the end of docks damaged by winter ice and spring ice thaw. We have installed several systems for your neighbors in Maine. I've enclosed a list of a few satisfied customers who have agreed to show you their systems, if you are interested.

You requested our price guidelines. For basic installation, which includes all hardware, our fee is $23.50 per square foot. Each dock requires installations on each side. A typical 12-foot dock, therefore, costs about $564 to keep free from ice damage forever. I'm sure you'll agree that the benefits exceed this low price.

Please call us to discuss details. It will be our pleasure to answer any questions or arrange a meeting at your marina to discuss your particular situation.

Sincerely,

Scott Admiral
Free Docks Enterprises
49247 Falmouth Road
Yarmouth, ME 04921
Encl

September 8, 2004

Basil Rathbone
Good Times Marina
448Ocean Way
Camden, ME 05482

Dear Mr. Rathbone,

Thanks for your interest in our de-icing system. Free Ducks offers a patented system that guarantees the end of docks damaged by winter ice and spring ice thaw. We have installed several systems for your neighbors in Maine. I've enclosed a list of a few satisfeid customers who have agreed to show you their systems, if you are interested.

You requested our price guidelines. For basic instullation, which includes all hardware, our fee is $23.50 per square foot. Each dock requires installations on each side. A typical 12-foot dock, therefore, costs about $654 to keep free from ice damage forever. I'm sure you'll agree that the benefits exceed this low price.

Please call us to discuss details. It will be our pleasure to answr any questions or arrange a meeting at your marina to discuss your particular situatin.

Sincerely,

Scott Admiral
Free Docks Enterprises
49247 Falmuoth Road
Yqrmouth, ME 04921
Encl

March 22, 2002

Benjamin Siemens
A-Plus Used Cars
73 Hyland Hill
Springfield, MO 52481

Dear Mr. Siemens,

As part of the disposition of my husband's estate, I have two lightly used vehicles that need to be sold. One is a Ford Explorer, 1999, with 65,450 miles, in perfect condition with lots of extras. The other is a 1998 Cadillac only used to for our winter trips to Florida. It has 45,672 miles and looks brand new. I have enclosed photographs.

I am now residing in Ohio and would like to have these cars sold. Are you interested in purchasing them for resale on your lot? If you would like to see the vehicles and make an offer that includes removing them to your lot, please contact my son, Robert, at 815 947-9002. I am sending this letter to three other dealers in town, so your quick response would be in your favor. I know that friends of my late husband bought good cars from you and that he would appreciate your honest reputation regarding his cars.

Sincerely,

Rita George
Encl:

March 22, 2002

Benjamin Siemens
A-Plus Used Cars
73 Hiland Hill
Springfeild, MO 52481

Dear Mr. Semens,

As part of the disposition of my husband's estate, I have two lightly used vehicles that need to be solded. One is a Ford Explorer, 1999, with 56,450 miles, in perfect condition with lots of extras. The other is a 1998 Cadillac only used to for our winter trips to Florida. It has 45,276 miles and looks brand new. I have enclosed photographs.

I am now residing in Ohio and would like to have these cars sold. Are you interested in purchasing them for reasle on your lot? If you would like to see the vehicls and make an offer that includes remving them to your lot, please contact my son, Robert, at 851 947-9002. I am sending this letter to three other dealers in town, so your quick response would be in your favor. I know that freindof my late husband bought good cars from you and that he would appresiate your honest reputation regarding his cars.

Sincerely,

Rita Peters
Encl:

December 2, 2004

Santini's Towing Service
Tony Santini, Owner
76 Brooklyn Parkway
Rosedale, NY 17382

Dear Mr. Santini,

This letter serves as notice that your loan account is 90 days overdue. If you do not pay off the loan amount on your account #WT908361, for the purchase of a 2003 Chevrolet tow truck, serial number TYP88900334, with a balance remaining of $18,934, by January 4, 2005, repossession processes will be instituted for said vehicle.

Please contact us at your earliest convenience to discuss this matter and advise us of your intentions.

Sincerely,

Robert Antonio
Credit manager
Rosedale Credit Union
1821 Barrington Avenue
Rosedale, NY 17323

December 2, 2004

Santini's Towing Service
Tony Santini, Owner
76 Brooklinn Prkway
Rosedale, NY 17382

Dear Mr. Santini,

This letter serves as notice that your loan account is 90 days overdue. If you do not pay off the loan amount on your account #WT9809361, for the purchase of a 2003 Chevrolet tow truck, serial number TYP88900433, with a balance remaining of $17,834, by January 4, 2005, repossission processes will be instatuted for said vehicle.

Please contact us at your earliest conveneince to discuss this matter and advise us of you intentions.

Sincerely,

Robert Antonio
Credit mnager
Rosedale Credit Union
1821 Barrington Avenue
Rusedale, NY 17232

Letter, Page 312

November 12, 2004

Jason Collier
Anderson Asphalt Company
2196 Jackson Avenue
Biloxi, MI 82364

Dear Ms. Collier,

This is to confirm our conversation of November 10 at the Radisson Hotel conference about scheduling the repaving of our company parking lot. Thanks for accommodating our desire to complete this job during the Christmas week shut-down of our factory. You also thought you could recommend a subcontractor to paint in the lines for parking spaces. I'd appreciate it if you would send me that contact information by return mail, John.

Here are the details I promised to send to you. Our parking lot is 200 x 350', for a total of 60,000 square feet. You quoted us a price of $5.50 per square foot, including the removal of existing pavement and preparing the surface for new asphalt. The price we agreed on is $358,000. You agreed that work would begin on December 26, 2004, estimated to be completed in four business days.

If you can confirm the above dates and costs on a contract to be received by us before November 23 and schedule your crews accordingly, we will send you the agreed upon 10% deposit of $58,500 by December 20, 2004. Jackson Ball Bearings looks forward to doing business with you.

Sincerely,

Stewart Jackson, Vice President
Jackson Ball Bearing Company
673 Collier Street
Biloxi, MI 86206

Letter, Page 313

September 8, 2003

Beverly Crawford
Miami Humane Society
3947 Sunset Street
Miami, FL 47261

Dear Ms. Crawford,

Thanks for your phone call last week regarding the purchase of 185 doses of distemper vaccines and 210 units of heartworm medication. We are pleased to inform you that we can accommodate your order at the discount price discussed.

Please sign the attached contract and confirm quantities, prices, and requested shipping dates. Return it to us **promply** to reserve your order. Because **vacinations** must be refrigerated, please allow an extra three days for the carrier to schedule a shipment.

Our company will also send ten boxes of our new flea preventative with your order at no extra charge. It is our pleasure to support animal shelters in their important work. Thanks for the opportunity to serve you.

Sincerely,

Althea Day
Fido's Healthcare Company
2131 South Harvard Road
Stanhipe, OH 57248

Letter, Page 314

April 23, 2003

Carol Dexter
Nova Services
29 Parkside Drive
Toledo, OH 59723

Dear Ms. Dexter,

I have noticed a discrepincy on the bill we received from your company dated April 19. The amount charged for Sandra **Morirty** for two weeks of temporary receptionist services exceeds our contract by $75.

Sandra worked for a total of 60 hours. Our contract states that her hourly rate would be **$6**.25. However, we were billed at an hourly rate of $8.10, for a total of $510.00. The contracted total was **$453**.00.

Thanks for checking into this for us, Carol. Upon receipt of a corrected invoice, we will send payment.

Sincerely,

Suki Yoshuri
Accounts Payable
Good Hands Insurance
34**83** Tower Way
Emmaus, PA 2**76**43

Letter, Page 315

September 4, 2002

Jose Perez
Peterson's Flooring Emporium
583 Hudson Avenue
Peekskill, NY 12749

Dear Mr. Perez,

Your services were recommended by a friend, Sadie Lamb, who was a **custemer** several years ago. We admired the tile your company provided and installed in her home. We have tried to match it in our local area, without success.

Sadie can't remember just when the work was done, nor does she have the receipt that might give details about ordering the tile. We hope that your records might provide the missing **infirmation**. We provide Sadie's address and telephone number to help you find her in your files. She is happy to confirm her agreement to this process, if you want to contact her.

Sadie **Jenkins**
73 Elm Street
La Grange, NY 12643
(212) 555-3**874**

If you can identify the tile that went into Sadie's house and had it in stock or could order it, we would love to discuss the det**ia**ls of purchasing it from you. We hope you can help!

Truly yours,

Bob and Linda **Jenkins**
389 Freedom Drive
Farmington, NY 12543

Letter, Page 316

March 11, 1999

Sarah **Peevey**
Sunny Acres Farm
91 Farm Ridge Road
Blaine, **MI** 64931

Dear Ms. Peavey,

As you may know, Saddle Up Stables in Blaine are for sale. I am considering buying the property as a **baording** and lesson facility. In my long-distance discussions with the current owner, your name was mentioned as a possible source for quality hay.

I anticipate that I would require between 7,200 and **8**,400 bales a year. The loft at Saddle Up will hold a month's worth, or about 600 bales. Would your **feilds** provide that amount of hay **annualy**? Would monthly delivery and unloading be **possible arrange**?

If the answer is yes to these questions, I'd be happy to speak with you about establishing a relation-ship. I'll be out of the country until the end of April. Please contact me at the **adress** below to let me know if you are interested. If not, do **you any** other local hay producers who might be? Thanks in advance for your time.

Best,

Lonnigan **Brody**
92 Cambridge Street
Malden, MA 02**865**

Letter, Page 317

May 2, 1998

Candid Camera **Shop**
Customer **Srvice** Department
89 Holly Corner
Granville, IL 34185

Greetings.

In 1989, I purchased a Nikon 335mm SLR camera from you, with a very special telephoto lens made in Denmark, for photographing tiny things. I specialize in Victorian **minitures**. The camera took marvelous photographs for 10 years. Sadly, I dropped the lens and cracked it. I'm hoping it can be **repired**.

I have inquired in my local area, but no one seems to have **axxess** to parts or service for this lens. I'm hoping that you do. It's a **Biorklund 9700**, 400mm lens. I'm happy to ship it to you from California, where I now live, if your service **teem** can help. Can you?

Sincerely,

Arthur **Togginberg**
236749 Pacific **Buolevard**
Del Coronado, CA 92618
(674) 845-19**98**

Letter, Page 318

April 14, 2003

Fins and Shells Seafood Company
ATTN: **Marc** Delrio
24 Ocean Blvd.
New Bedford, MA 02634

Dear Mr. Delrio,

We here at the Community **Vocationl** College are excited about the graduation **lambake** your company has agreed to cater for us on June **6** this year. To confirm our conversation earlier this week, here are the details.

We are expecting 52 graduates and **401** guests, as well as 25 **faclty** and staff. To feed these **131** people, you advised that we would require:

250 pounds of clams,

250 stuffed quahogs,

200 ears of corn,

100 pounds of potatoe salad,

25 pounds of green salad,

75pounds of Indian pudding,

and 50 pounds of vanilla ice cream.

Your company will also provide soft drinks, **bttled** water, coffee and tea for the gathering. Your staff will arrive at 10AM on June **9** to set up the food in time for the 2**AM** clambake. The bake pit will have been dug for your staff in advance. By 5PM that day, your staff will have completed the clean-up.

We will send a deposit of $2,**53**4, half the contracted price, upon receipt of a written contract from Fins and **Sm**ells.

Thanks in advance for your excellent service and food.

Sincerely,

Barbara Jones
Events **Coordinater**
CVC
3472 Fairhaven Rd.
Fall River, MA 02573

Letter, Page 319

September 8, 2004

Basil Rathbone
Good Times Marina
448Ocean Way
Camden, ME 05482

Dear Mr. Rathbone,

Thanks for your interest in our de-icing system. Free **Ducks** offers a patented system that guarantees the end of docks damaged by winter ice and spring ice thaw. We have installed several systems for your neighbors in Maine. I've enclosed a list of a few **satisfeid** customers who have agreed to show you their systems, if you are interested.

You requested our price guidelines. For basic **instullation**, which includes all hardware, our fee is $23.50 per square foot. Each dock requires installations on each side. A typical 12-foot dock, therefore, costs about **$65**4 to keep free from ice damage forever. I'm sure you'll agree that the benefits exceed this low price.

Please call us to discuss details. It will be our pleasure to **answr** any questions or arrange a meeting at your marina to discuss your particular **situatin**.

Sincerely,

Scott Admiral
Free Docks Enterprises
49247 Falm**uo**th Road
Yqrmouth, ME 04921
Encl

Letter, Page 320

March 22, 2002

Benjamin Siemens
A-Plus Used Cars
73 **Hiland** Hill
Springfeild, MO 52481

Dear Mr. **Semens**,

As part of the disposition of my husband's estate, I have two lightly used vehicles that need to be **solded**. One is a Ford Explorer, 1999, with **56**,450 miles, in perfect condition with lots of extras. The other is a 1998 Cadillac only used to for our winter trips to Florida. It has 45,**276** miles and looks brand new. I have enclosed photographs.

I am now residing in Ohio and would like to have these cars sold. Are you interested in purchasing them for **reasle** on your lot? If you would like to see the **vehicls** and make an offer that includes **remving** them to your lot, please contact my son, Robert, at **851** 947-9002. I am sending this letter to three other dealers in town, so your quick response would be in your favor. I know that **freindof** my late husband bought good cars from you and that he would **appresiate** your honest reputation regarding his cars.

Sincerely,

Rita **Peters**
Encl:

Letter, Page 321

December 2, 2004

Santini's Towing Service
Tony Santini, Owner
76 **Brooklinn Prkway**
Rosedale, NY 17382

Dear Mr. Santini,

This letter serves as notice that your loan account is 90 days overdue. If you do not pay off the loan amount on your account #**WT9809361**, for the purchase of a 2003 Chevrolet tow truck, serial number TYP88900433, with a balance remaining of **$17,834**, by January 4, 2005, **repossission** processes will be **instatuted** for said vehicle.

Please contact us at your earliest **conveneince** to discuss this matter and advise us of **you** intentions.

Sincerely,

Robert Antonio
Credit **mnager**
Rosedale Credit Union
1821 Barrington Avenue
Rusedale, NY 17232